# Mindfulness and Meditation

The Mindfulness solution to detox your mind, recovery and renewal therapy

(A Beginner's Guide Finding Happiness and Peace Through Meditation)

**Van Richmond**

Published by Rob Miles

© **Van Richmond**

All Rights Reserved

*Mindfulness and Meditation: The Mindfulness solution to detox your mind, recovery and renewal therapy (A Beginner's Guide Finding Happiness and Peace Through Meditation)*

ISBN 978-1-990084-11-9

All rights reserved. No part of this guide may be reproduced in any form without permission in writing from the publisher except in the case of brief quotations embodied in critical articles or reviews.

## Legal & Disclaimer

The information contained in this book is not designed to replace or take the place of any form of medicine or professional medical advice. The information in this book has been provided for educational and entertainment purposes only.

The information contained in this book has been compiled from sources deemed reliable, and it is accurate to the best of the Author's knowledge; however, the Author cannot guarantee its accuracy and validity and cannot be held liable for any errors or omissions. Changes are periodically made to this book. You must consult your doctor or get professional medical advice before using any of the suggested remedies, techniques, or information in this book.

Upon using the information contained in this book, you agree to hold harmless the Author from and against any damages, costs, and expenses, including any legal fees potentially resulting from the application of any of the information provided by this guide. This disclaimer applies to any damages or injury caused by the use and application, whether directly or indirectly, of any advice or information presented, whether for breach of contract, tort, negligence, personal injury, criminal intent, or under any other cause of action.

You agree to accept all risks of using the information presented inside this book. You need to consult a professional medical practitioner in order to ensure you are both able and healthy enough to participate in this program.

# Table of Contents

INTRODUCTION .................................................................. 1

CHAPTER 1: TESTING YOUR OWN AWARENESS ................. 3

CHAPTER 2: WHAT IS MEDITATION? .................................. 8

CHAPTER 3: INTRODUCTION TO MINDFULNESS ............... 19

CHAPTER 4: IMPROVING YOUR MENTAL HEALTH WITH THE RIGHT FOOD AND SLEEP .................................................. 26

CHAPTER 5: MORE TECHNIQUES FOR DEALING WITH STRESS .............................................................................. 35

CHAPTER 6: EFFICIENT WAYS TO IMPLEMENT STRESS MANAGEMENT .................................................................. 45

CHAPTER 7: GENERAL FORMS OF MEDITATION ............... 64

CHAPTER 8: MINDFULNESS MEDITATION EVERYWHERE . 86

CHAPTER 9: MEASURE STRESS ......................................... 91

CHAPTER 10: PREPARATION AND STARTING MINDFULNESS MEDITATION ..................................................................... 97

CHAPTER 11: THE SIGNS YOUR BODY SENDS YOU: STRICT DIETS AND COMMON CONDITIONS .............................. 122

CHAPTER 12: STEPS TO MINDFULNESS ......................... 146

**CHAPTER 13: LIVING IN THE MOMENT** ............................ 155

**CHAPTER 14: LIVING IN THE MOMENT** ............................ 162

**CHAPTER 15: HOW TO STAY MOTIVATED TO DO MINDFULNESS MEDITATION** .......................................... 169

**CHAPTER 16: MEDITATION ON THOUGHTS** .................... 177

**CONCLUSION** ................................................................. 200

## Introduction

Many people ask, "How can I live more in the moment?" Unfortunately, most people do not find a sufficed answer for that question.

The busy world we live in today is chockfull of worries and troubles that make living in the moment increasingly difficult. The cacophony of anxiety and self-consciousness that accompanies such a busy life makes discovering how to live in the moment more expedient. Knowing how best to deal with the never-ending stream of thought of past mistakes and future uncertainties to think and worry about may be difficult.

This book outlines a systematic journey towards discovering how you can live life as it happens and enjoy the things that matter the most to you. We will be looking into the magic of deep breathing, more so, how this simple technique helps you deal with anxieties as well as worries of past or future events.

We shall also discuss other techniques that will help you attain an increased level of relaxation and focus.

Thanks again for downloading this book, I hope you enjoy it!

## Chapter 1: Testing Your Own Awareness

Your sense of observation

There will be those among you who cheat but remember that if you do cheat, it will take you longer to understand what mindfulness is all about. I cheated but advanced beyond that because the only person I was cheating was myself. Find somewhere to sit that is unfamiliar to you. This could be in a park. It could be in a room at work, but the best results are always gained from being close to nature. Take a quick look around you and then close your eyes.

What is it that you saw when you looked around? Describe in your mind's eye what exactly you saw. Were there clouds in the sky? Were there flowers and if so what color were they? Was there a predominant color? Was there something particularly beautiful in your surroundings? Were there any people? Go into as much detail as you can, in your mind's eye.

In a TV show, people were presented with a whole chain of items passing them on a conveyor belt. They were permitted to keep those items if they could memorize them all but of course there were many that missed their attention. In your case, you must describe everything you saw before opening your eyes to reveal the reality. People tend to miss things. There may have been obvious things that you should have included in your mental image of that place, but that you omitted. The reason for this is that you haven't yet trained your mind to be in that moment in time and aware of everything around you.

This book will show you how this is accomplished because until you learn to be centered in the moment, you cannot gain all of the benefits from your experience. It will take a little time to get accustomed to, but the journey will be worth the while.

Observing people around you

Observation of people around you helps you to get things into perspective. Look at how happy people attract friendship and how sadness tends to turn people away. People who learn from observation of others really can decide how they want to appear within any given space of time. They become aware of their inadequacies and work toward making themselves the best person that they can be in any given situation.

What does that mean?

That means that your sense of happiness is vital to good health, to good feelings within yourself and to those around you. If you feel uncomfortable with your situation or yourself, you tend to give less to the moment. Look at how people interact. Think of which activities you would prefer to avoid. Perhaps, by observation, you can see where people go wrong and you may have some of these failings yourself.

The confidence that you gain from mindfulness is amazing. Look at confident people. Their demeanor is different to that of people with less confidence. Note their body language. It's not a question of how they look from a point of view of actual physical beauty, but how they feel on the inside. Some people are more mindful than others and aware of the way that they interact with others. These are people who are happy and content and who can walk into a room and turn heads without even trying. Their appeal is the calmness of their demeanor and the happiness they show which is overflowing and completely natural.

You learn a lot from observation and in the next chapters, we will walk you through mindfulness exercises that will help you to live in the moment and make that moment the best one you ever lived. Mindfulness is about being aware that this moment in time is all that you have and this awareness makes you fill that moment with contentedness because otherwise, the moment is lost forever and becomes a lost opportunity.

Above all else, mindfulness is awareness of yourself in everything that you do, but these exercises in observation will help you to see what to recognize in yourself in order to improve what you see. Mindfulness is not judgmental. It's simple observation and contentment with self and once you start on this practice, you will find that all the gifts life has to offer will present themselves to you and that you will be extremely happy and content.

## Chapter 2: What Is Meditation?

They say the mind is a muscle. It can be trained, developed, and pumped like biceps or triceps. Including teaching new skills. Concentration, the ability to concentrate, to keep mindfulness is among such skills. For their development, we use meditation.

Meditation is a method of developing clarity of mind, clarity of perception of the world, and intuition. Meditation helps to improve interaction with our emotions. The flow of thoughts, to come to an understanding of how we live, what are the true reasons that guide our actions. And most importantly, meditation teaches us to manage it all.

"Meditation" is an ancient word that has its roots in Latin: "meditari" means to reflect on, observe, and consider. In many parts of the world, this practice has existed for more than 5,000 years. Before this word was corrupted by religions, spiritual practices, different teachers, esotericists, and mystics, this process was understood as a way to develop the mind. Its ability to focus on a particular object or action and to be less affected by emotions, pain, suffering, and other states, body, and spirit.

It is important to note: there is no religion or religiosity here. None at all. No mantras, chants, dances, or whatever. All of this tinsel is to the side. It distracts from the point.

The development of the spiritual principle often becomes one of the side effects of meditation, without being its goal. From the rich historical experience, it is well known that religion and spirituality are not synonymous. Sometimes it happens that representatives of religion are far from spirituality, and lies, lust, intolerance, and fears are manifested in their actions. Sometimes stronger in ordinary people. "Ordinary" people are sometimes much more spiritual than religious people, although followers of religions claim to have a monopoly on spirituality. It is not necessary for a person to be religious in order not to steal; it is enough to realize that theft causes damage to others and destroys the identity of the thief. Meditation increases the level of awareness of actions and their influence on the world around us. This is why meditation becomes an important spiritual means of development.

By practicing meditation on an ongoing basis in our rather busy lives, we have the opportunity to improve our mental and physiological state. This is not an allegation, but the results of many studies conducted over the past 40 years in the best research institutes of the United States (Harvard, Stanford, University of California, etc.). Meditation is used not only by a huge number of professionals (doctors, therapists, consultants, trainers) but also by an even greater number of "ordinary people" - such as you and me.

There is only one problem with meditation today - there is a huge amount of speculation, tinsel, oddities, nonsense, and ambiguity around this word and the technology itself. It is enough to refer to Wikipedia to see all that number of different, sometimes contradictory statements, doctrines, and definitions.

It will probably be easier to approach the question of what meditation is, defining what meditation is not:

Meditation is not "going into astral" or anywhere else from the body.

Meditation is not an entrance to a trance or a different state of consciousness.

Meditation does not set a goal to change the state of consciousness.

Meditation is not an escape nor departure from reality.

Meditation is not a way to relax.

Meditation is not something mystical or secret, available only to "initiates."

Meditation is not only for those who profess Buddhism, Hinduism, or something else Eastern, or Indian, or esoteric or mystical.

Meditation is not "thoughtlessness" or "insensitivity."

Meditation is not a way of self-hypnosis.

There are a lot of delusions, but if you think about it, it will become clear - they are all based on the postulates that are unknown from now on or on scraps of words, phrases taken out of context, statements or advice of those who really understand little in meditation: I have never tried it, or use these errors for my own, often selfish purposes.

Meditation is a simple, special exercise for the mind.

And that's all. Simple? Yes. Another thing is that it is in this incredible simplicity that the whole complexity lies.

There are many different ways to meditate. They differ in a point of concentration fire, breath, counting, body, text, sound, phrase (mantra), sensations, some visualization, or any other external object (for example, a wall). There are active meditations, dance, or chaotic movements. And there are also passive meditations, motionless sitting, lying down or standing. What do all these practices have in common besides the word "meditation"? There is always a certain object of concentration. Yes, there are religious meditations, but they are used in the appropriate context of the relevant religious doctrines. And there is also something in them that they focus attention on. In Christian practice, it is prayer, in Muslim practice dance, in Judaism reading.

The goal of any meditation is to create conditions for the mind in which it will be maximally focused on any one object. If everything is so easy and simple, what is the problem?

Meditation does not have a very good reputation. It is one thing to say that I do badminton, not to mention skiing or judo, and quite another to say: "I do meditation." You can hear in response: "You, what, yogi, or what?." And this can happens in many countries in the minds of people. This process is still too closely connected with Eastern religions. Meditating, a person seems to cross a certain line and not only trains the mind but takes the path of foreign spiritual practice. In other words, separates from the others, from the "normal" mass. This is an interesting observation. Almost all publications where articles on the topic of meditation are published are devoted either to yoga or to a healthy lifestyle. At the same time, they are all focused exclusively on the female audience or on the part of the male audience that is identical to the female in the perception of the editors of these journals.

The conclusion is simple: meditation in the view of many is not serious, and normal people do not need it. This is superfluous, there is no time for this, there are other more important and useful things. Yes, and money must be earned. And then you need to rest. To go to the cinema, to read different things in the social network, to see the news, and a lot of things. Not to sit like an idol, idle. The result we live on. Do not strain.

The fact that sometimes we are not satisfied with ourselves, our life, our actions, nothing, we are not guilty, this how the world is. The fact that the brain lives on its own, rushing from side to side, from Facebook to YouTube and back through Twitter is nothing. The fact that it is hard to keep attention on one case is believable. From all this, we often have difficulty sleeping. You can always strain, gather strength, spend more time, or accept the situations and sleep. This is what we often do, instead of the living, and it had lead to an automated lifestyle. Peculiarly more like robots than thinking living beings. This is not a big deal, and we have to tolerate it. However, there is good news.

The meditative state, the state of concentration of attention, is inherent in many people and far from religious activities. When we do one thing at a time, are fully focused on it, and are aware of it, then such a process is meditation. Cycling or skiing. On a snowboard? Running? Climbing the mountains? Badminton? All still would! Judo? Generally impossible without meditation!

Creativity is a separate topic. The creation of any work leads to a state of consciousness very close to the meditative one. Focused peace. Maybe meditation, in its deepest essence, is trying to be like the act of creation?

When in the silence of the apartment, there is only a quiet scratch of the silver-lit laptop keys, and in the background, headphones (if early in the morning) or from the stereo system (if in the evening) play your favorite music. And the letters are folded into words, and the words are in sentences, when everything except for the simplest, but powerful word processor, it is turned off. And nothing distracts, and the mind flows forward line by line, then. The clarity of perception of reality increases, smoothly, confidently, steadily.

Do a pleasant job and realize that at the same time, another process happens — the process of spiritual growth. Creativity is no less meditative than sitting in meditation. Behind the facade of words, inside the process is the same filling. Sit down and write a poem, cook and drink tea (and if you follow the Chinese tea ceremony ... but more on that later), draw a picture, listen to your favorite melody, walk in the park, race at high speed along the slope. You should feel every note of music, every subtlety of a syllable, every nuance of the taste of tea - and there will be an aftertaste, light, and tart, maybe sweet, maybe milky. Become the process itself its nothing but a single action and is clear, deliberate, complete.

No religion. Simply. Clear. Easy. From here, you can begin to come to understand meditation as a phenomenon. Meditation is a development of the process of creativity, or rather, that part of the process that is associated with a concentration on the object of creativity.

## Chapter 3: Introduction To Mindfulness

Being the central tenet of Zen Buddhism, mindfulness deserves a deeper understanding from a theoretical and a practical perspective.

Mindfulness is the state of allocating one's consciousness to the present time and current physical space. It is not different from when our parents told us to be mindful of what we were doing when we were kids. Mindfulness is a simple concept with deep consequences.

Anyone can start on the path to becoming mindful and anyone can take it at his or her own pace. The concept has proven to be so successful, that even western psychology is seeing the benefits of using mindfulness exercises for a wide array of mental illnesses.

If you can understand the concept of the mind, then the benefits of mindfulness is obvious to you. Let us look at some basics, and then dive into how mindfulness works.

The Basics

We are surrounded by the present. That present is measured in terms of time. We are also surrounded by physical space. Across two dimensions, we are standing at the juxtaposition of our own unique space and time. The spot that you are standing on belongs to only you. It is your unique point in space. The time you occupy that space, is also uniquely yours.

The second thing you should take a moment to think about, is the consciousness that envelopes you. What is your consciousness? It is that feeling and notion that gives you a sense of self. You are reading this book, and you know you are. This consciousness is more than just your heartbeat, pulse, gastrointestinal activity, pulmonary activity, even brain activity. Your consciousness is a lot more. Consciousness can be described, in part, with the perception of your self-awareness. Mind you, self-awareness is not all about consciousness. It's only a part of it.

When you practice mindfulness for a short amount of time, you will feel the ability to peel your awareness apart from your physical self and be able to look at things from a perspective that your body does not care about. In mindfulness exercises, all forms of vanity and desires are cast aside, but not in a direct sense. They are cast aside by virtue of a state of mindfulness tying the present time and space, to the consciousness and renders everything else irrelevant.

How to Invoke Mindfulness

Mindfulness is not the same as meditation (although meditation is a natural extension of it). Meditation requires a static location where the person sits down in private and enters the state of meditation. When the session is over, and the person departs the location, the meditation, and the effects that flow from it, cease. In mindfulness however, it is distinctly different. In mindfulness, the practitioner can continuously remain in a state of mindfulness without abdicating the benefits that it harnesses.

Peace and happiness are not the product of mindfulness. They are the natural extension of it. It is as clear as noon is, when the sun is at its zenith.

To invoke mindfulness, begin in seclusion and slowly build your skills until it can be invoked anywhere, anytime, and for however long. After practicing, The question then becomes, why would one not want to be in a state of mindfulness?

Steps to Mindfulness

The steps to mindfulness are straightforward. It requires the practitioner to mind one thing at a time and all else will fall in place. To get started, choose a room in your home where you will be free of all disturbances and interruptions. As much as possible, remove anything that will disrupt any of your five senses. Some practitioners include scented candles and incense sticks. Stay away from that and keep the room as fresh and quiet as possible. If you are easily distracted, find a room where even light can be kept to a minimum. In the dark, without any sound and smell, you should be alone. The aim at this beginning stage is to create an environment that leaves you only to the sound of your mind and nothing else.

Once you have the room set-up, find a comfortable position and sit in a way that will not tire you after a few minutes of stillness. Each person's body is unique and thus, each person's posture is unique. Find yours over time. For now, it is acceptable to sit on a recliner, with your feet up and your arms at your side.

Once you are in your position and you are ready, close your eyes and let a few moments pass. Let your breathing stabilize and do not make any effort to control it. Let your central nervous system do what is necessary to get your oxygen levels all sorted out and it will regulate your breathing to a state of rest.

Once you are in a state of rest, begin to monitor your breath. Monitoring your breath is very different from controlling your breath. Do not control your breathing. Do not increase its rate or depth. Just watch your breathing in total silence. At this point, do not measure, count, tamper with it. Your only task at this point is to watch.

In a state of rest, you will notice that your breathing is extremely calming. One of the many uses of breathing (aside from supplying oxygen to your lungs and expelling carbon dioxide), is its ability to be almost hypnotic due to its rhythmic nature. The longer you are able to focus your attention on this breathing of yours, the more peaceful things around you will get.

For the next few days, keep practicing this technique of watching your breath flow in and out. Keep doing this, for at least a week. While you are doing this, do not anticipate or expect the next step. If you are expecting something to happen, that is the antithesis of mindfulness, because expectation means that you are transcending your current space and time and placing your thoughts in a point in time that is not the present. Do not expect. Just perform.

## Chapter 4: Improving Your Mental Health With The Right Food And Sleep

What's key to understand here is that it's not just our thoughts that lead to these changes. Just as important is our biology and our lifestyle and our bodies and minds exist in a tightly linked cycle of activity.

For instance, when you eat this results in an increase in serotonin. Why? Because foods – especially carbs – contain an amino acid called tryptophan. When blood sugar increases, the body responds by releasing insulin which triggers the absorption of glucose from the blood to be used for activity or stored as fat. But tryptophan does not get absorbed and as such, it remains in the bloodstream. This then gets circulated to the brain, where it is converted into serotonin – that's because tryptophan is a precursor (building block) for serotonin.

This is why your mood tends to improve when you've eaten. And this then results in the release of ghrelin to signal that you're getting fuller and to prevent you from over eating.

Later on, that serotonin converts into melatonin – the sleep hormone. This is why everyone falls asleep after Christmas dinner! That melatonin reduces activity in the brain and this then triggers the release of other inhibitory neurotransmitters like GABA.

Did you know that darkness also triggers the release of melatonin?

And meanwhile, the longer you stay awake, the more adenosine (another inhibitory transmitter) builds up in the brain. This is partly what gives us 'brain fog' after a long hard day because it is a by-product of the energy process used in brain cells.

What all this means, is that after a long day and big meal, you are sure to start getting tired at the end of the day and find it harder to wake up and do something productive. That's not you being lazy or disinterested, that's you being at the whim of your biology.

Now let's say that we want to wake ourselves back up. What do we do? One simple option is to go outside or shine a bright light – sunlight triggers the release of cortisol, which along with nitric oxide will help to wake us up. This is why we should avoid looking at phone screens when we're getting ready for bed.

Or how about jumping in a cold shower? This stimulates the release of epinephrine, norepinephrine and testosterone – waking you up and making you much more focused. It's the adrenaline that causes the hairs to stand up on your body.

Loud noises can create enough shock to wake you up and so too can hunger. When we're hungry, we have low serotonin in our brains which in turn increases the cortisol – stress hormone – ratio. That's why we get anxious when we're hungry and it's why some people also get 'hangry'.

There are all kinds of other interactions like this that can have a huge effect too. For instance, as pain is linked with anger, this explains why we're cranky when we have aches and pains. It also explains why if you keep flicking your dog's ear, it will eventually turn around and bite you...

Making Use of Your Biology

So what can we take from all this?

For starters, it's useful to recognize the role of your natural ebbs and flows and your biology. In other words, try not to get too alarmed if you find your-self feeling very stressed or very tired. Likewise, try not to let anger cloud your judgement. Often we will shout at our loved ones when we're angry or stressed partly because our perception of events has changed and had negative slant. We might even find ourselves thinking things like 'all they do is take advantage'.

Remember: that's angry you. That may well simply be the result of cortisol, of testosterone or of all three. Try not to put stock in what you're thinking.

This also means you can 'fix' your mental state in all manner of ways. You can wake yourself up with a cold shower and some blue light (blue light being the term used to describe light with the same wavelength as the sun). If you're in a bad mood, then you should try to increase serotonin which you can do with food – or more sensibly by increasing vitamin C. Something else that triggers the release of serotonin is exercise! This is what causes what we know as the 'runners' high'.

If you want to perform at your very best, then use this information to try and improve your sleep. This will help you to wake up with your brain feeling far more refreshed and with much less 'brain fog' slowing you down and making you groggy.

Another tip is to sync your routine to these natural rhythms. If you're going to feel tired and content after a meal, then it's important to make sure that you've already done everything you want to do before you sit down to eat.

Want to be more productive in the evenings? Shift dinner back half an hour! Likewise, recognize that you're less likely to be productive straight after you've eaten at lunch. Conversely, if you're going to try and think creatively – do it when you're relaxed and calm.

Combating Stress

Also useful to know is that you can use your body to calm stress and event eliminate what would otherwise be a panic attack. That's because our sympathetic nervous system – which controls our fight or flight response (as well as our opposite 'rest and digest response') – is tightly linked with breathing and heart rate. When you breathe quickly, it makes you more stressed and increases your heart rate.

Conversely though, if you breathe more deeply and more heavily, this helps to encourage a much calmer response and puts you more in the rest and digest state. Breathing deeply is thus one of the best ways to calm yourself down and one of the best ways to prevent serious anxiety.

How to Upgrade Your Mental Energy

What's more important of all though, is that you ensure you have the right diet and that you are in good shape. This will transform the performance of your brain by drastically increasing the ability to create neurotransmitters as needed and by increasing the amount of energy your brain receives.

One way to do this is to consider using some form of multivitamin tablet. This should contain vitamins like B12 and B6, which are used to supply the brain with energy as well as to help create a large number of neurotransmitters. Also used in the creation of many neurotransmitters and hormones are vitamin D, vitamin C, magnesium, zinc and more. If you make sure you are getting these in your diet, then you will find it easier to switch from being highly focused to being relaxed and creative and you will find your brain lasts longer before getting tired. Also particularly important is choline, which is a precursor to acetylcholine found in eggs – this can help improve your sensory perception, your alertness and your memory all at the same time! Amino acids found in protein are also critical for a wide range of neurotransmitters.

Other nutrients that are very important are those that improve the energy and function of the brain. Any vasodilators for instance, such as garlic, will help to get more blood and more oxygen to the brain helping you to stay alert for longer. Creatine is a bodybuilding supplement also found in red meats and this is great for reducing adenosine and also increasing mental energy – studies show that this alone can be enough to boost IQ! Omega 3 fatty acid improves cell membrane permeability, which means that neurons are better able to communicate with one another. Exercising regularly will help you to create more neural connections in your brain, increasing your ability to learn via heightened plasticity (and brain derived neurotrophic factor). This will also increase your body's energy efficiency and help you to experience less stress.

In short, it is highly important to eat a nutrient dense diet and to train hard if you want to perform at your mental best. Get more nutrients and substance, avoid junk food and 'empty calories' (which spike the blood sugar and throw our entire system out of whack), sleep well, run and lift weights.

As you do this, your brain will instantly start to become hardier, more efficient and less groggy on the whole. And your performance and productivity will also grow to reflect that.

## Chapter 5: More Techniques For Dealing With Stress

We all face different kinds of stress in our life. It enters in and out of our lives on a daily basis - and it can quickly walk all over us unless we take action. Luckily, there are many things you can do to diminish and manage stress. Here are some techniques you can deal with stress without creating more stress and trouble.

Find the roots of your stress

When we are stressed, it seems like our stressors are coming from every angle around us. We are overwhelmed, and we take a defensive position and not a pleasant one at that. Rather than being in the dumps, find out the reasons why you are feeling stressed. Is it because of work, exams, a conflict with your supervisor, household chores, a fight with your significant other? When you get specific and define the stressors in your life, you are placing yourself in a better position to plan and take action.

Focus on what you can control

While you cannot control what your boss does or what your in-laws say or what your friends do, you can control how you respond, how you do your work, how you devote your time and what you use your money on.

One of the worst things you can do when you feel stress is trying to control uncontrollable circumstances. Why? Because when you will inevitably fail for it is beyond your control. Doing this will only make you feel more stressed and helpless. However, you can identify the stressors that you can manage and determine the best methods to eliminate them.

Follow Your Heart

It's so easier to cope with stress when you are doing things you inevitably love. Think about it for a second. If you wanted to be a painter growing up, how many times will you stress out over art compared to a desk job? One of the best ways to reduce and eliminate stress is to divert your attention away from your stressors and focus on the things you are passionate about. What hobbies do you enjoy doing? What hobby helps relax your mind? If you're not certain, test with a variety of different activities until you find something that's significant and enjoyable.

Manage your time.

One of the most popular stressors for people is lacking in time. In this busy world, we are overwhelmed with chores, our to-do-lists, work-related duties, our studies, etc. We all wish we have more time on our hands to complete everything we need to get done. Time can utterly lead us to stress out even more. For example, if you have to finish a project by a certain date, thinking about the amount of time you have left can make you feel under pressure. Luckily for you, when you practice mindfulness you ignore the fact of the many minutes you have on your hands and solely focus on the task in front of you. Now there are only 24 hours a day, how you utilize your time will determine how productive you will be and how stress you will feel.

Understand that worrying is not helping.

Sometimes our thinking patterns can promote stress so that a small triviality can turn into a pile of stressful situations. We all believe the worrying can be productive, or at least the proper response to stress. But we overlook worry for a solution to our stressors. Instead of worrying, take action. Find ways on how you can eliminate or reduce the stressors in your lives.

Finding Happiness in Life

What do you want out of life? Most will say they want to find happiness. So, how do we find happiness in life? To find true happiness in life, you will need to work on yourself and make a few modifications to the way you live your life. These methods are actually straightforward, and if you perform it right, you will reach this kind of authentic happiness most people spend their lives pursuing. In this chapter, we will discover ways to find happiness for yourself.

Don't count on other people to make you happy.

If you trust that other people to make you happy, that will give you constantly disappointment. One of the most popular reasons why most people feel miserable in their lives is because they assume others to give them things that they can only give themselves. Consider it for a second. If you frequently outsource duties of filling emptiness and finding happiness, you will never be truly happy. Rather, you will be at the pity of everyone you meet.

Only you can measure how happy you are and how you think about yourself. Quit accusing others for producing your feelings. Place yourself in charge and accept responsibility for your own happiness and your sense of pride.

Stop being envious of others.

Envy is one of the most negative characteristics a person can seize. As you go on in life, you will surely bump into people who are wealthier, more charming, funnier, and more confident than you. But you shouldn't care at all. People who appear to look like they are perfect and ahead of you are lacking characteristics as well. Nobody is perfect. You cannot be happy if you are yearning to be someone else, it will only make you sad and cynical.

Be genuinely happy for others.

If a friend you know abruptly becomes rich, be actually happy for them! They did not take something away from you, and they probably fought just like you and most people do on the journey to reach their dreams. If you work hard and never give up, you will achieve the same award. Keep in mind, if you try to shatter this person's accomplishments, you will not improve any of your life circumstances.

Show kindness to all.

Unhappy people are known to be nasty, malicious, rough, mean, and rude to lots of people. Happy people feel fantastic about oneself and life in general. They also wish to brighten other people's day as well. Doing acts of kindness makes a synthetic feeling that makes you feel good, positive, and confident in yourself. You can do little things, such as smiling at people or giving up your seat on the bus, or powerful things like volunteering and donating. You should also withdraw gossiping. While it may appear to be fun, no one ever gets any positive vibes from tormenting someone else.

Be grateful.

Happiness isn't about holding your wants, but desiring what you have. Most of us have grown accustomed to focusing on all the problems we are facing in our lives, rather than anything remotely positive. We all crave for a better career, a better bond with someone, better buddies, a better form and a better home, anything better to improve our circumstances. We always focus on what's absent from our lives and neglect what's right there in the presence of us. To be truly happy you must practice gracefulness and change your mentality to be thankful for everything you have.

Accept the things you cannot change.

There are numerous things you cannot change about life. You cannot change your lifespan, you cannot change your appearance, you cannot change what someone else thinks, you can't change the past, and you cannot change the world. All you can do is live in the present and move forward and do your best not to duplicate the same errors. Do not spend your energy and time thinking about what a worthless life you have. Rather, focus on what you have now and how you can improve these characteristics to reach your goals.

Let Go of Grudges.

Stop holding grudges on other people and yourself. Whenever you carry grudges, you are only wrecking yourself. You are allowing negativity to run through you, and you're keeping yourself stuck in unpleasant past experiences. Forgive others wrongdoings and let it go. Maybe you believe they didn't earn your forgiveness. But forgiving others is always better than suppressing feelings of hatred and hostility, and it is only beating you more than it is them. Stop holding grudges, forgive others, and move on with your life.

Take care of yourself.

When people's circumstances have changed for the worst, they will remark how poorly they've been treating themselves. They sleep at weird hours; they eat unhealthy food, they lay on the lounge watching countless hours of TV, they forget to shower. Truly happy people take care of themselves. This means the more you take care of yourself, the more happiness you will be able to draw. Schedule time for exercise; make an effort to eat healthily, take pride in your appearance. Exercise and healthy eating goes a long way to change the way you feel about yourself and will provide you an inner luminosity that shines outside.

Watch the people around you.

The people in your life will surely have an influence on you. When it comes to friends, quality is always better than quantity. Remove all the negative people in your life who bring you down. Spend more time with positive, optimistic, and bright friends who see the good in you and will lift you even higher.

## Chapter 6: Efficient Ways To Implement Stress Management

Deal with Your Stress

Stress is known to be one of the most widely recognized reasons for ailment in our general public today, thusly you have to figure out how to deal with your stress. Stress is in charge of the breakdowns seeing someone at work, school and at home which at that point lead to health issues Learn how to limit, lighten or wipe out stress in your life. It is presently perceived in the business field that stress-related issues are one of the most widely recognized reasons for non-appearance in the work place.

Significant Corporations are currently perceiving the need to deal with your stress and are executing stress decreases programs in the work place. Stop and check out what's going on in your life right now.

Deal with your Stress in regular day to day existence. Observe the things that happen each day that directly affect your stress levels. Before we can manage the issues that stress makes in our lives, we have to perceive and comprehend what is happening, see what exists and after that build up an arrangement and treat the fundamental causes.

Stress is all over. Regardless of whether you are a worker, a chief, jobless or an understudy, you experience a wide range of stress in your life. Whatever your calling or status throughout everyday life, you can't flee from stress. In any case, there are approaches to adapt to the stress. Stress management incorporates approaches to manage the day by day weight of life. With the correct disposition, you can carry on with a without stress life in the midst of your stressful condition.

Distinguish the Sources of Stress in your Life

The underlying advance in stress management is to know the wellsprings of stress in your life. Albeit a few sources are inescapable, you can make approaches to decrease them. In any case, if the wellspring of your stress is avoidable, attempt to discover approaches to keep away from the stressful circumstance with the source.

Due dates

The standard wellspring of stress from work and school works is complying with the time constraint. Be it a report or a task, it is sufficient to give you stresses. A viable stress management in gathering due dates is to take a shot at the undertaking as right on time as could be expected under the circumstances. When you get the undertaking, attempt to take a shot at it the soonest conceivable time to avert a propensity for continually beating the due date. Along these lines you can even have additional opportunity to survey your work, coming about to unrivaled reports and papers.

Pointless Responsibilities

Another regular wellspring of stress is the point at which you acknowledge obligations that are beyond what you can tolerate. Successful stress management shows individuals how to state no. By just disapproving of obligations, you lessen the measure of stress in your life. Nobody can say what amount is sufficient. Anytime you believe you can't offer time to an additional duty, saying no is the best alternative.

Learn Healthier Ways to Manage Stress

A few people manage stress by smoking, crying, gorging or undereating and drinking excessively. Despite the fact that this may happen now and again, consistent utilization of these methodologies will cause you more stress than any other time in recent memory. When you anticipate stress or experience it, attempt different stress management systems. Take a walk, have an exercise custom, write in your diary or play with your pet. These are healthier approaches to stress management. Utilizing the systems, you calm your stress without hurting your body.

Managing stress proficiently is the way to endure an incredible requests. By learning stress management, you can all the more likely adapt to it. You possibly have two choices with regards to this, it is it is possible that you stop the stress or the stress will murder you. It is your decision and you should make the correct one.

Stress Management - A Healthy Lifestyle Equals a Healthy Workplace

Stress can have hindering consequences for an individual's body just as their life. Stress brings down the insusceptible framework, in this way debilitating the body's guards. The individual turns out to be increasingly vulnerable to numerous conceivably hazardous afflictions.

The impacts of stress shift from individual to individual. One individual may build up a moderately sensible sickness, for example, a gastrointestinal condition, while others may encounter all the more conceivably hazardous illness, for example, hypertension or coronary illness. Contingent upon exactly how much stress an individual is encountering, a few conditions may emerge all the while. This is the reason legitimate stress management ought to be learned and rehearsed consistently.

There are numerous approaches to actualize stress management into one's life. One route is by recalling not to take work home. Regardless of whether you work out of your home, it is critical to isolate office time from individual time. Permitting an adequate measure of time every day to appropriately loosen up and unwind is an extraordinary stress management strategy. Investing quality energy with family, perusing a decent book or cleaning up are extraordinary approaches to decrease stress.

Exercise is another brilliant stress management strategy. There doesn't need to essentially be any sort of formal exercise program, just fusing strolling, biking or notwithstanding cultivating into your life will do the trick. Also, the more pleasant the exercise, the more viable it will be. Many pick yoga as a strategy for stress management. This is a particularly brilliant decision since yoga isn't just physical however it likewise includes the mind and soul all in all. Whenever rehearsed all the time, this can be exceptionally recuperating for the body.

Some of the time the most valuable strategy for stress management is just keeping stressful occasions from occurring in any case. For instance, a work environment could hold an obligatory reoccurring meeting to enable all representatives to voice their sentiments about how things are going and to give criticism. This avoids stress by empowering everybody to talk about issues that may have been irritating them and potentially resolve the issues.

One more approach to counteract or diminish the measure of stress in the work environment is by guaranteeing that there are sufficient representatives to finish assignments in a sensible timeframe. At the point when laborers are surged and need to comply with almost outlandish time constraints all the time, this puts the representatives under a lot of weight, which could bring about expanded sicknesses. It is significant that businesses cling to this, in such a case that a lot of their workers are out on wiped out leave, there will be next to no profitability.

On the off chance that businesses have positively no decision yet to push their representatives to comply with a significant time constraint, at that point an appropriate method for giving stress management during this period could be offering paid downtime and rewards to compensate the diligent work. On the off chance that this kind of stress management can't be used, at that point maybe an elective method for loosening up after such a stressful time can be utilized.

Legitimate and normal stress management should be fused into the lives of everybody, regardless of whether they are a housewife with three kids or a CEO of a noteworthy organization. Stress management isn't significant for a healthy way of life, yet additionally to improve proficiency at the work environment.

The Easy Stress Management Techniques

These are amazing methods that are anything but difficult to learn and they don't take a great deal of time or exertion. As soon as you notice you don't have opportunity to tune in to a guided unwinding CD, or take an interest in an exercise program or ponder for 30 minutes every day, at that point these procedures will give you a brisk method to start to battle the impacts of stress. No reasons, everybody possesses energy for this stuff so how about we get the chance to work!

Procedures I - Just Breathe!

I have individuals approaching me always for straightforward stress management methods to bring some relief. Let's be honest, we are pushing ahead at a pace today that overrides anything in mankind's history. What's more, if I'm not mistaken, we are not doing so well. Simply read the most recent insights with respect to our health in this nation and the pattern is stunning. We are accomplishing more with less assets and attempting to fit it all in at a completely rankling pace...something must give! All the most recent data and investigation demonstrates to us that the conventional everyday stress in our lives is in charge of 66% of every one of specialists' visits! People, that is everything from the basic cold to coronary illness and malignant growth, and if stress isn't the essential driver of the issue, it is absolutely a contributing component.

I know from individual encounters the impacts that stress can have on the body and our emotional wellness. By a wide margin the most significant stress management strategy I generally show individuals initially includes basic relaxing! I recognize what you are thinking...you are as of now breathing throughout the day. Genuine, however the majority of you are doing everything incorrectly!

I will watch my associates while they are composing, seriously centered on some venture. Their breathing is so shallow it's astounding they can even support their life! Not exclusively is their breathing shallow, yet it is additionally for the most part finished with the upper chest. This isn't an effective method to inhale and it loots the collection of valuable oxygen. Presently I don't think about you, however I'm truly excited oxygen is without still and since I'm not paying for it I'm going to take in as much as I can. With regards to breathing you can spend lavishly and be insatiable!

Legitimate breathing starts in the stomach. The stomach goes about as a cries in the body and as it grows it maneuvers air into the lungs. Filling the lungs appropriately will furnish you with astounding outcomes in decreasing stress. All that oxygenated tissue will help each procedure of the body including your capacity to center, digest sustenance, and loosen up muscles, just to give some examples. And for all intents and purposes, each part of your physical and psychological well-being can be improved with legitimate relaxing.

How about we investigate how we can take an appropriate breath. Put one hand on your chest and your other hand on your stomach. Presently take in a full and complete breath, filling your lungs with however much air as could be expected. When you have got done with breathing in at that point breathe out, keeping your hands set up. Take another breath and this time give close consideration to how your hands move. What you're going for is to have the hand on the stomach move outward from the body first as the lungs load up with air. As more air fills the lungs then the advantage should move outward from the body as your chest extends. When you breathe out the hand on the chest should move in before the hand on the stomach and you ought to breathe out completely and totally.

I would prescribe you take 40 full breaths consistently. Incidentally, don't do this at the same time except if you appreciate feeling faint, I don't need you hyperventilating and going out! I like to pick something to remind myself to relax. Ordinarily, I watch the clock and that can make me begin to feel stress as solid pressure coming into the body. Thus, every time I wind up checking the time, I interruption to take a full diaphragmatic breath. I additionally utilize this method when the telephone rings, so before I answer I have taken a full breath and felt a flood of unwinding wash over me. It truly causes me plan for whatever I might confront. This additionally functions admirably for those occasions I feel that outrage going ahead because of the day by day open doors for self-awareness and development my multi year old girls' dramatization brings into my life.

You can't locate a simpler system that can accomplish such a great deal for controlling stress. Attempt this for yourself for the following week. Make the promise to change this one part of your life and you will start to see the intensity of straightforward stress management strategies. To a limited extent two of this article we will investigate the intensity of setting a positive expectation

Systems II - Shake it, Shake it!

One of the most widely recognized territories of the body where we will in general hold stress is the strong framework. Stress can make the muscles actually contract and fix, regularly prompting fits and genuine torment. Most of individuals feel this pressure in the upper back and neck and they can encounter everything from a mellow consuming sensation to weakening agony. Frequently, this is the antecedent to pressure cerebral pains and it can truly upset our lives.

The greatest issue with strong strain issues is to get the issue before it shows itself as solid torment or cerebral pains. The most concerning issue with this is it very well may be hard to anticipate when this will happen in light of the fact that the torment appears to simply abruptly show up. Be that as it may, it is conceivable to figure out how to feel the strain sneaking in on the off chance that we simply give more consideration to our bodies. In this way, we should investigate how to actually shake that pressure out!

Alright, stand up, give yourself a lot of room and attempt this examination. Start to tenderly shake your correct hand at the wrist. Attempt to seclude only the wrist as you let the pressure start to shake out. Your fingers ought to be free and floppy. Keep in mind, this is a delicate shaking; you are making an effort not to win a challenge here. Do this for around 15 seconds or somewhere in the vicinity and afterward incorporate the lower arm up to the elbow as you keep on shaking. Once more, attempt to let the strain simply wash away as the arm is truly free and floppy. Proceed with like this for an additional 15 seconds. At that point incorporate the entire right arm, as far as possible up to the shoulder. Everything in the arm is free and floppy now as you delicately shake away any staying strain. Make an effort not to oppose at all and see exactly how free you can make the muscles in your arm. Do this for an additional 15 seconds and afterward stop.

Presently simply let your arm hang down. Look in a mirror and you if you have done this accurately your correct arm will be recognizable longer than the left! You may likewise see a beating or shivering sensation in your fingertips and your hand may even feel warm and flushed. This is on the grounds that you have freed yourself of the choking strong strain that was available in the arm and blood and vitality are presently streaming all the more effectively enabling the arm to feel progressively loose. You have truly shaken the pressure out of the arm and in doing this have stepped toward loosening up your body and dealing with your stress.

You will need to rehash this on the opposite side of the body so you have balance. You can do this in the legs also, beginning with the foot and lower leg and stirring your way up the leg until it is all shaking. When doing the leg shaking it is a smart thought to relentless yourself on a divider or seat so you don't free your equalization. You many need to consider a private spot to shake out the strain except if you need some weird looks and conceivable undesirable consideration! Obviously, if you do this in a bank on a Friday evening, you are ensured to move ideal to the front of the line!

Alright, since the arms and legs are free, you can move to some delicate shoulder shrugs, neck turns and some other developments and delicate extending that you like to do to help release the storage compartment muscles. On the off chance that you are composing or stuck at a work station throughout the day I prescribe doing these exercises about once an hour to keep the pressure under control and you can do them as frequently as you like consistently. Simply make sure to keep everything delicate, free and loose and clearly stop if you feel any torment or unsteadiness.

Presently you are along the way to lessening solid pressure. Allow it to shake, shake and roll.

## Chapter 7: General Forms Of Meditation

Your research on the internet might have made you think that everybody is practicing meditation. However, with plenty of information available concerning the subject, you can easily get confused about how you should meditate. This is because there are various ways of meditating. It is therefore crucial that you invest your time in researching more about the forms of meditation available. Luckily, we have done the research for you. This chapter will outline for you some of the most popular meditation strategies out there. With the help of this information, you should select the technique that best suits you.

Buddhist Meditation Techniques

Vipassana Meditation

Vipassana is a Pali term which refers to the idea of seeing things clearly.[6] (The Pali language is a language native to the Indian subcontinent.) The meditation technique stands as one of the oldest forms of meditation which was utilized in India. The method was popularized by the Vipassana movement and S.N. Goenka.[7] Vipassana meditation is also referred to as insight meditation.

How to Do It

Different teachers have varying ways of teaching the meditation technique. Nevertheless, we will focus on the most common way of engaging in this form of meditation. During the first phase of the meditation practice, one is required to be mindful of their breath. The importance of this step is that it guarantees that the mind is stabilized and that total concentration is achieved.

The next step is to build clear insight. Emphasis is placed on being aware of your mental state and bodily sensations. It is required that one should be conscious of what is going on around them. However, you should not hang on to any thoughts or sensations. For beginners, the following example should help them understand how this form of meditation works.

Start by finding a comfortable place to sit. This can be sitting on the floor or on a cushion. In your sitting position, ensure that your spine is erect and your legs crossed. If you choose to sit in a chair, avoid leaning forward or backward; instead, sit upright. The first step is what is referred to as the samatha practice. This is the step where you develop the art of concentration. Basically, concentration can be achieved through mindfulness breathing.

Your breath is the point of focus of your meditation. All your attention should be centered on following how you breathe. From exhaling to inhaling, your mind should strictly follow this movement. While breathing in and out, you should notice how your body movements are affected by your breathing. Your abdomen is rising and falling.

As you spend more time focusing on your breathing, you will realize that other sensations and perceptions are fading away bit by bit. The sounds that you once heard are slowly disappearing. Your emotions are also parting off from you. Briefly, take note of these happenings as they open your door to self-awareness. Now, return to your state of breathing. All your attention should be on how you are breathing. Everything else should be classified as noise.

From the Vipassana meditation technique example discussed, you realize that there are two things that your mind can be drawn to. First, the primary object or the key object of focus is breathing. The secondary object of focus is what could be referred to as "noise." Anything else which tends to deviate the mind from the primary object is noise. These are your perceptions such as external sounds, body itchiness, smells, feelings, memories, etc.

When the secondary object pulls at your attention, you should not resist. Rather, you should embrace what is happening. Focus for a moment on what is swaying your mind from the main object, then bring back your mind to the key object, your breath. When your attention is pulled to the side, you should strive to label what you are experiencing. What is it that is deviating your attention? Label it. It could be thoughts, desires, sounds, or memories. The process of labeling what you are experiencing is identified as "noting."[8]

The significance of noting is that it gifts one with the ability to note thoughts, feelings, and anything else that could deter them from thinking clearly. Giving these items labels helps to confirm that you are not easily carried away. What happens is that you realize that the noises are only passing through you. So, you are kept in a state where you are fully aware of what is going on. Ultimately, you build an art out of clearly seeing things as they are without allowing them to affect you. Hence, the term Vipassana.

## Zen Meditation

This form of meditation is also referred to as Zazen meditation. It is a Japanese type of meditation with its roots in ancient Chinese Zen Buddhism.[9]

## How to Do It

Zen meditation is also commonly known as seated meditation. Therefore, this technique is done when one is sitting down. You can choose to sit on anything as long as you are comfortable. If you are sitting on the floor, your legs should be crossed. However, if you prefer sitting in a chair, the most important position is to ensure that your back is straight. Your mouth should be shut with your eyes lowered. Your stare should be on the ground and slightly in front of your feet.

The concentration of your mind can be attained by either focusing on your breath or just sitting (a practice called shikantaza[10]). If you choose to focus on your breath, your attention should be centered on how you are breathing. This means that you should be mindful of how the air is coming in and going out of your nose. To give this a boost, you should count the number of breaths you are taking. Remember, this is something that your mind should be doing to move it toward a state of awareness. Start counting from ten as you move backward. You may get distracted as you continue counting. When this occurs, you should gently prompt your mind to start again.

If you opt to use the shikantaza way, the idea here is to remain conscious of the present. It is worth noting that there is no object of focus used here. One should be fully aware of what is happening at that very moment. This means taking note of how you are feeling and the thoughts coming in and out of your mind. While this is happening, you should not cling to anything.

## Mindfulness Meditation

Just like Vipassana, mindfulness meditation was also derived from ancient Buddhist meditation. This form of meditation also features influences from other traditions such as Zen Buddhism from the Vietnamese. John Kabat Zinn pushed for this technique in the West. He is credited with launching the Mindfulness-Based Stress Reduction (MBSR) program in 1979. The program has since been used in a number of hospitals.[11]

## How to Do It

The major aspect of mindfulness meditation is that the practitioner ought to focus on the present. While doing this, they should be non-judgmental with regards to thoughts going in and out of their minds.

The sitting position should be upright. This can either be done on the floor or on a chair. Your back should remain unsupported if you will be using a chair.

Mindfulness meditation also requires that you should be mindful of your breath. This implies that as you breathe in and out, you should be conscious of your body movements. Depending on the length of your meditation, you should maintain the right posture while making sure that your attention is on your breath.

Moreover, attention should also be placed on the sensations and thoughts which will be going on. Efforts should be targeted toward existing at the moment without allowing distractions to swerve your mind. This doesn't mean that you won't be distracted. However, it is crucial that you are cognizant of the fact that you are being distracted. Your mind can be slightly distracted, but you should strive to bring it back into the actual picture and continue focusing on your breath. The point here is that you should not be part of the feelings going on around you. Rather, you should only be aware of their existence and their effects on you.

Another way of practicing mindfulness meditation is by applying it to your daily activities. For anything that you do, you should do it mindfully. Whether you are walking, eating, or talking to others, mindfulness meditation can be practiced anywhere If you are eating, there is nothing else that you should be doing. The same case applies to your conversations. If you are talking to your partner, be present at the moment without allowing your mind to be distracted.

If you are still new to the world of meditation, this technique can be a great way of getting started. You only need to make sure that you are aware of what is happening around you. It is crucial to get understard that this is not Buddhism. Rather, the meditation technique only uses Buddhist practices because of the perceived mental and physical health benefits.

Metta Meditation

The term Metta is a Pali term which means goodwill, loving-kindness, or friendliness.[12] The meditation technique is derived from ancient Buddhist practices, particularly the Tibetan and Theravada lineages. Just like the name suggests, this is a method which helps one to empathize with those around them. Equally, it aids in the development of compassionate feelings, both toward your inner self and toward those surrounding you. With the help of this method, one gains a sense of purpose of their life and an overall boost in self-acceptance.

How to Do It

The first step would be to assume a meditation position. Next, the practitioner should use their heart and the mind to generate good feelings of love and kindness. This begins by first generating kind feelings about yourself. Thereafter, this is extended to include others. In other words, the sequence should progress from yourself, followed by your close friend, then another neutral person, then to a rather difficult individual to deal with. Finally, this attitude should be developed toward the universe.

Generally, the idea here will be to evoke a mindset where you wish the best for other people. Practically, this can be attained by reciting affirmations which bring these good feelings about yourself and to those around you. The more often you do this, the more you will realize that you will be happy.

If you are looking to improve the relationships you have with other people, then this technique will suit you. Likewise, if you are facing a situation where you think that you are just bitter about yourself, then the Metta meditation will serve you best. It will help bring positive vibes into your life.

Hindu Meditation Techniques

Transcendental Meditation (TM)

This is a type of mantra meditation which was pioneered by Maharishi Mahesh

Yogi.[13] The method was first introduced in India in 1955. Many Beatles fans may have heard of Maharishi. He garnered fame during the late 1960s for mentoring the celebrated rock band and the Beach Boys. Transcendental meditation is practiced globally due to its immense benefits. Scientific research has also been conducted on the technique to prove its associated health perks.

How to Do It

Transcendental meditation has a price tag as it is not offered for free. Therefore, for you to experiment with this technique, you have to hire a licensed instructor. Nevertheless, with the vast support that the method has, you can be sure that you will be getting value for your money.

In this form of meditation, a mantra is used to help you concentrate. You may be wondering what this "mantra" is. Well, these are just sounds or words derived from the Vedic customs, which is one of the major traditions in India that shaped

Hinduism.[14] When engaging in this practice, one should concentrate for about 20 minutes. It should be practice twice daily.

Supporters of TM argue that this form of meditation takes the mind through a transcendent state. This state is then replaced by a state of self-awareness. As such, the meditator will have gained perfect stability, rest, stillness, and order.

Several studies on TM have revealed that it is beneficial in helping people deal with high blood pressure, chronic pain, cholesterol, and anxiety.

Mantra Meditation

Basically, this method uses a mantra to help bring your mind to a particular focus. The mantra chosen can be any word that you connect with. The word or phrase chosen doesn't have to mean anything. It will only help you focus. When using a phrase, it is imperative that you settle for something that is easy to recite without causing any distractions. More importantly, you should choose a phrase which inspires you.

How to Do It

When practicing mantra meditation, the first step is to choose a word or phrase that you will use as your mantra. The second step is to assume a meditation position. You can choose to sit on the floor or in a chair. The important thing here is that you should be comfortable and upright. Your eyes should be closed, and you should monitor your breaths.

Once you have gained a still posture, you should recite your mantra slowly. Your attention should be on how you sound and how the phrase or mantra relates to you. The flow of the mantra should be in harmony with your breath.

After 10 repetitions, you should then move on to reciting the phrase with only your lips. This time around you should do it almost silently. The same recitation rhythm should be maintained. After another 10 slow and steady recitations, you can then take it internally. This is where your mind takes over the recitation without having to utter a word.

Thoughts will begin flowing inside your mind. While in an awareness state, you ought to understand that this has to happen. Gently return to your recitations to focus your attention again. At this stage, the sound in your mind should be the center of your attention.

The practice should continue for the designated amount of time that you were to meditate. When concluding the process, you should do this gradually. Begin by taking some deep breaths first and continue sitting calmly. Enjoy the quiet state and acknowledge the change that you are experiencing. In spite of what will happen, keep in mind that practice makes perfect. Hence, you should continue the meditation for the best results.

Yoga Meditation

"Yoga" is not a new term to most of us. This is a common form of meditation which we have often heard about. However, all that many of us know about yoga is that it is good for our physical and mental health. Most people have not taken the time to comprehend how it is practiced.

There are several rules of conduct which define how yoga should be practiced. In this case, a yogi should use the right postures, breathing exercises, and meditation practices. Yoga might be something that you came across over the internet; nevertheless, this is one of the earliest forms of meditation on earth.[15]

How to Do It

There are distinct forms of meditation which are exercised in yoga. Notable techniques practiced out there are as briefly discussed.

Third Eye Meditation

Basically, this type of meditation puts attention on a spot which is between the eyebrows, hence the name "third eye." The main reason for drawing attention to this spot is to ensure that the mind is silenced. As the meditator continues with the practice, they will notice their thoughts getting wider and eventually, they will achieve a quiet state of mind.

Chakra Meditation

In this form of yoga meditation, one gives attention to one of the body's centers of energy termed a "chakra." There are seven energy centers in our bodies. They include:

Muladhara -root chakra

Svadhistana -sacral chakra (linked to sexuality)

Manipura -solar plexus chakra

Anahata -heart chakra

Vishuddha -throat chakra

Ajna -third eye chakra

Sahasrara -crown chakra

Your aim is to focus on each by reciting a particular mantra for each center of energy.

Gazing Meditation

This method requires the meditator to fix their state on a symbol or any other external object such as a candle. Unlike other forms of meditation, it is also practiced when the eyes are open. At some point, the eyes should also be shut. This aids in developing the visualization aspect of the mind. Therefore, after your eyes are shut, the image you are focusing on should be in your mind. The mind's eye should have developed and internalized the image.

Kundalini Meditation

Kundalini meditation is a complex type of meditation. Essentially, it involves stimulating the kundalini energy. In yoga, this energy is perceived to rest at the bottom of your spine. Due to the complexities of this method, meditators should practice it with the help of a qualified teacher.

Kriya Yoga

This type of yoga brings together different types of meditation exercises which were once taught by Paramahamsa Yogananda, a yoga guru. The practices are more spiritual than other types of yoga. Therefore, if you are looking for spiritual enlightenment through yoga, then this is the right choice for you.

Sound Meditation

Simply put, this involves the use of sound to meditate. The yoga practice is also referred to as "Nada." Calming music is used to help soothe the mind to quiet down. With time, the student should be able to internalize the sound and listen to the sounds without any vibration.

**Tantra**

Unfortunately, Tantra meditations have gained a bad reputation in the West as they have the notion that this technique is more sexual. Nevertheless, the method goes deeper beyond just sex.

**Pranayama**

This yoga technique is not considered to be meditation. It is a way of regulating your breathing. The breathing practices are useful in helping the mind achieve total concentration. Combining the breathing skills acquired here with other forms of meditation will guarantee admirable results.

"I Am" and Self Enquiry Meditation

The basis behind this form of meditation is that it seeks to investigate the reasons behind our existence. In line with this, it strives to help you answer the question "Who am I?" It is from getting answers to this question that one garners a deeper understanding of themselves. The meditation method was hyped by Ramana Maharshi.[16]

Chinese Meditation Techniques

Quigong

Pronounced "chee-gong," this refers to an old Chinese healing technique and exercises which entail meditation, movement exercises, and controlled breathing.[17] Consequently, with this method, a student not only works on exercising their mind, but they also engage their bodies in physical exercises.

## How to Do It

An interesting aspect of Quigong is that there is diversity in it. There are many ways of engaging in the physical exercises required by the method. Equally, there are more than 80 varying breathing techniques recommended. Some exercises are done for healing purposes whereas others are essential for meditation and spiritual awakening.

## Taoist Meditations

Taoist meditations can be traced back to the 6th century B.C. Over time, the practices have been influenced by Buddhism and therefore they portray certain similarities.[18] The importance of these meditations is to calm the mind and the body with the purpose of uniting the body and the spirit. Overall, your body and spirit should be in harmony with the Tao.

## Chapter 8: Mindfulness Meditation Everywhere

Okay, so now when you know a little bit about the enemy within and what it's doing to us. How can we get rid of this little man who's running around in our head? I would not suggest that your first goal is to get rid of him. As you will find out his actually not that dangerous once you face him with the right mindset. The first thing to understand is that you decide how much power this little man is going to have. You are in control, remember that.

So the first this you'll have to do is to become aware. When you become aware, you create distance. There are a couple of ways to do this. The first suggestion I have for you is to sit down and meditate. Boring, you might say, we'll if you said that then you definitely need meditation. In the world today, we have become so addicted to constant stimulation. We leave no room to become aware. So leave your phone somewhere else, I even suggest turning it off. We'll that's dangerous, what if there's an emergency. When someone brings up this argument, then I ask them how people were able to survive before the phone was even invented. Anyways that's a different story.

Sit down in a quiet room, have your body in a position of dignity. Have your back as straight as possible. Begin to become aware of your breath, both your inhale and exhale. Where is your breath? Is it in your chest or stomach? Don't try to change it if it's in the chest just be aware of it. When your monkey mind begins to think of something else, just bring back the attention to your breath. Have full acceptance of what's going on in your body and mind. Maybe your mind begins to drift into thoughts of what you need to do, how this is stupid and you feel uncomfortable. Relax and bring your attention back to your breath. That's the mini person trying to control you. Don't judge him, focus on the breath. Do this for at least 5 minutes.

Make it a habit to begin your day with 5 minutes of focusing on your breath. Before you do anything, make coffee, eat a sandwich, whatever your morning routine is. Simply but your legs on the side of the bed and sit for 5 minutes in a straight up position. And remember, I can't stress this enough, have acceptance! Whenever you find yourself focusing on something else than the sensation of your breath, simply bring you attention back to it. The purpose of this exercise is to break free from the identification with your thoughts/mini person. Accept the sensation in your body. Don't label it as anxiety, begin calling in the sensation. It's not good or bad, it's simply a sensation.

When you do this, you'll find yourself becoming better and better at focusing on your breath. If you like the feeling you get from it, begin doing it longer than just for

5 minutes. The ultimate goal here is to bring the awareness of your 5 minutes in the morning to the whole day. So for example, if you're doing the dishes or walking outside become aware of your hands moving your breath, the sound around you. You now have a weapon against this mini person - awareness.

I'll share with you what I believe is the second most effective weapon towards this enemy within. Now this requires that you have created some distance first. The idea is to use humor. If you've ever watched south park or another TV-show or movie that has a character with a voice or style that you can't take seriously. Simply adopt those characteristics on to your mini person. So whenever he is telling that you that you can't do this, you're feeling this, you're afraid of this, etc. You think of this character that you can't take seriously saying all these things.

Key takeaways:

- Awareness is the most effective weapon towards the enemy within/mini person. Begin every day with 5 minutes of meditation where you focus on your breathing.
- Begin to become aware in situations of your daily life. Bring your attention back to the now.
- Whenever you feel as if your voice is taking over. Adopt the second most effective weapon, which is humor. Adopt characteristics to the mini person that you can't take seriously. Remember you are always the one in control.

## Chapter 9: Measure Stress

The path to being more mindful begins with time away, experienced teachers, and scientific validation; it becomes something you can practice right now with a powerful exercise.

Wherever you are, whatever you are doing, measure your stress level. 10 is our level of stress in a catastrophic accident. 1 is our stress level when we just woke up from a perfect nap.

How high or low is your stress level? As you read, you probably feel a little bit stressed, maybe a two, three or four. Any time we pay attention we experience stress.

Stress doesn't have to be a bad thing; it is your brain responding to where you are, what you do, or what you think. If you weren't feeling a little elevation of your stress hormones, you couldn't pay attention to these words.

Now, try a short experiment. Imagine your favorite place in the world. Close your eyes and stay in the image of that place for a few moments to a few minutes.

What is your stress level?

It probably went down to a one or two. It can't be zero because you're not dead. The alarm in our brain is always on to protect us from bears, even when we sleep. What's so powerful is that you just switched your brain from a more to a less alarmed state by measuring stress then choosing what you wanted to think about.

In a lab at the University of Indiana, Professor Cara Wells has shown that the dendrites of our pre-frontal cortex shrink under stress. Those same neural pathways that grow with mindfulness shrank when her animal subjects experienced chronic stress or exposure to the stress hormone corticosterone. This is why the first mindfulness exercise we all need to use is measuring our stress level.

The value of using measurement has been further proven with fMRI. Cognitive behavioral therapy (CBT) works on a simple premise: even though we think we can use reason to change our behaviors, whether those behaviors are painful thoughts (like self-doubt or depression) or unhealthy actions (like eating whole pizzas), we often can't.

One of the most powerful CBT techniques is self-monitoring. Just as noticing anxiety and naming it turns down the alarm, brain imaging research shows CBT techniques can switch the brain from anxious to calm. What the alarm demands is mindful attention to its signals. When we mindfully measure our stress level, we discover the true character of the experiences in our lives, both those we crave and those we want to change.

The evidence is persuasive that noticing your level of stress on a consistent basis achieves three very important goals: it provides evidence to your alarm that you care about its signals; it stores memories about what experiences and behaviors create stress and the happy and calm moments we want more of; and finally, measuring stress allows us to choose what we want to experience in our lives.

To emphasize the experience of measuring stress, I need you to try a less pleasant second experiment. Think of the person you least enjoy right now: a co-worker, a family member, or a pesky neighbor.

Imagine them for a few seconds.

Again, measure your stress level. How high did it go? Your brain is so powerful you can merely think about a person you don't like and it raises the level of stress hormones. Your alarm knows this person is a threat, real or imagined, and it wants you to be ready to deal with the potential trouble.

But that's absurd. The person is not a bear. They aren't with you right now. There is no reason for your stress level to rise.

This is the reason measuring our stress level is the first mindfulness practice too few of us take advantage of. If we can't separate real stress from the stress we create or that which our brain creates when it doesn't need to, we are constantly stuck in a cycle that removes choice from our lives.

Instead of choosing how we want to spend each moment, we react to our circumstances. When we are unconsciously stressed, our brain reacts, trying to keep us safe. We aren't in the moment; we're on the roller coaster of wherever our brain wants to take us that removes us from the perceived danger.

When you are at a stress level of seven, eight, nine or ten, you are intense, ready to spring into action. That's not bad if you're on the football field on game day, but it is absolutely unhelpful when you try to relax with someone you love. Stress creates behaviors that don't reflect our values, what we really think and feel.

The moment you measure stress, while you may not like the feeling, you are wherever you are. Suddenly, we can feel the calm or heightened chemicals in our body. When we measure how stressed we are on a regular basis, we can uncover why our levels go up and down.

Measuring stress doesn't instantly make us a Buddha or solve all the problems that create stress. What it can do is open up our brains to whether we have the life we want or whether we need to do more mindfulness exercises. The more exercises we do, the more connected, attentive, and nimble our brains become.

## Chapter 10: Preparation And Starting

## Mindfulness Meditation

As I told you before, developing mindfulness takes time and effort, but when you become mindful you will see that is worth it. And probably you have already read about how to gain mindfulness on the internet and you have seen posts that say that you can become mindfulness in a short time and without any effort, but how? Nothing in the world, even the simplest thing to achieve, has its difficulties and of course a real time to achieve it. That is why I am not going to fill your head with exercises that will help you develop mindfulness in a "short" period of time. We are going for the reality and for the real meditation.

Meditation is not easy for everyone, especially if you haven't done it before. However, it gets easier as you progress and go further into it. Also with the true information about meditation you will meditate easily in no time. But, before going on with the meditation, you should first get the base knowledge of it. The base is important; because everything that is built in life is based on how strong the base is.

Prepare for mindfulness meditation

Right now all you need is the road map for your journey. The preparation and the knowledge for meditation is the road map, and now you will get it. Once you get it and you follow that map you will be meditating before you know it.

Prepare yourself

Before getting into any kind of meditation practice it is very important to know that the practice you will be doing is not a performance. You should never evaluate the practice as a "bad" or "good" meditation. If you are thinking that meditation is performance –based you have missed the point totally. The goal in the practice is simply to learn.

For instance, if you are taking the breath as the object of attention, then the goal is not to hold the breath for too long, the point is to learn how it is to pay attention to the breath. If you notice that your mind starts to wander too many times, even more than you have expected, it means that your mind is really busy. If it wanders only on one topic, try to learn why that specific topic is on your mind. If you find out that it is really a lot on your mind, then you will know what you need to pay attention to and later on what to focus on to resolve the issue.

Everyone's mind usually wanders, even people with over 50 years of experience in meditation wander. This is a very intriguing topic to talk about, that is why you will learn later more about this, because it is an important part of meditation.

Don't forget your heart

There are so many ways people teach mindful practice, however, in the way that

I am about to tell you is more effective. It is simple, but most of the other teachers forget to say it. Never forget your heart. This attention to the heart releases tenderness and curiosity to the practice.

When pain is involved, you are aware of the pain and this type of attention has its own wanting to be supported. Put it in another way, it is self-compassion and also self-care.

In other words, you have started to read this book and now you are prepared to start the practice. You have even tried the beginner's exercises, this means that you care about yourself, and you are now aware that the practice will be a gift for you and to the people around you.

Forgive yourself

Like all of us, you will be imperfect at this. If the time passes and you have forgotten to practice, then practice "Forgive-Invite". Forgive yourself for the time that passed. Do that by investigating what was the thing that took you off course. Next, while you are aware invite yourself to start again.

You can take this as a forgiving practice; you can begin any time and to be present in your life to your life again. It will take you only a moment.

Thank yourself

One of the most important part about meditation practice is to thank yourself when you do it. When you are finished with the meditation, you recognize yourself for putting in this effort and the time you have taken out from your busy life, of course for your own good, learning, well-being and health.

This will be imprinted into your memory; you care enough about yourself so that you have paid attention to yourself. Your self-compassion type of energy will start to heal fast. What will the months, weeks and days be like if you just have this incredible energy running in your body and mind?

Remember to come back to these 4 essential elements when you practice your meditation.

Find a friend

These 4 elements that we have discussed, can be practiced on your own, however if you like you could have someone join you. Maybe you know a person who is also interested to start the practice of mindful meditation. If not, ask the people you know well and present to them what mindfulness is all about, you might get their attention and they will join you. Also, you can find out if there are groups near you that practice mindful meditation or a group that is ready to start.

Finding a buddy to practice mindfulness is not essential to start with, however, if it makes you more relaxed and connected to others than it is a good thing for you. It can also help your motivation.

Myths about mindful meditation

There are so many rumors about mindful meditation and how it supposed to be practiced. You can never know which one to follow and which one to believe. That is why I decided that is important to know the top myths about meditation.

Myth 1

Mindfulness is to take some time-out from your life, to reduce stress and to quiet your mind

This is the number one myth that is spreading between people that practice mindful meditation and those that want to start. This is how some people are experiencing this practice. The real thing about mindful practice is to wake up to the inner work of your physical, emotional and mental processes, and to recognize the connection between people; to operate with higher compassion towards yourself and others.

Myth 2

You need a lot of time to find the "mindful" space

As I have told you before, mindfulness can be practiced in different ways. Your personal life and circumstances will tell you what works for you. There isn't one right way to do it. It will become a tug of war if you are struggling to add meditation into your busy day. However, to marry meditation with life is all about balance.

There are so many people who are fighting to place mindful meditation in their lives. Just start with the basic meditation, like breathing. Also, adding other exercises, which you can do anywhere and anytime of the day. Just like the once I told you about.

Myth 3

It's about concentration or focusing

Yes, one of the benefits of mindful meditation is to be able to focus and concentrate, this practice is not about concentrating and focusing. Don't forget, mindfulness is all about cultivating awareness. Yes, concentration is an important thing for the well-being but it is not part of mindfulness.

You are sitting in meditation, focusing on your breath and stilling your mind, but your mind is wandering off. The fact that your mind is wandering never means that you are unmindful. It means that you are present and you are in the state of mindfulness. In other words you are sitting still and just observing the mind aware fully.

Myth 4

Mindfulness is for those who are relaxed

Usually people who are far from relaxed are starting the journey to mindfulness. But, as the time passes and with good effort to develop mindfulness, those people have gained a sense of control and also are able to go through their problems with ease. People that are restless are those who search for a way to calm themselves down and most of them find the right one, mindfulness. They gain all the benefits of mindfulness and soon they are no longer restless.

Myth 5

Those who teach mindfulness are always mindful

Wrong! Even the teacher with many years of experience and many years of being mindful are not always mindful. They can find themselves in many mindless moments. But, they have never given up when their mind wandered off. They forgive themselves and continue on their path. Maybe they are teachers, but they also got the benefits from being mindful. It has been helpful for them in so many ways, for their relationships, professionally, with the kids and for their physical and mental health.

Benefits of Mindfulness Meditation

Yes, mindfulness brings so many benefits that will make your life so different in so many good ways. However, meditation also brings additional benefits, especially if that meditation is for developing mindfulness.

With regular meditation, 20 minutes each day for a few weeks the benefits will start to appear. The benefits that you will get from mindful meditation are grouped in three ways: Emotional well-being, Mind developing and healthy body.

Emotional well-being:

- Reduced impulsivity, anxiety and worry
- Reduced depression, fear, stress and loneliness
- Higher self-acceptance and self-esteem
- Improved resilience to adversity and pain
- Increased awareness, relaxation and optimism
- Preventing emotional smoking and eating
- Developing positive connection with people
- Improved emotional and mood intelligence

Mind developing:

- Increased mental focus and strength
- Increased memory recall and retention
- Better creative thinking and cognitive skills

- Better problem solving and decision making
- Better process of information
- Helps in ignoring distractions
- Helps in managing ADHD

Healthy Body:
- Improved energy level and immune system
- Improved heart rates and breathing
- It will reduce blood pressure
- Longevity
- Less brain and heart problems
- Lowers asthma and inflammatory disorders
- Lowers menopause and premenstrual syndrome
- Helps in preventing HIV, Fibromyalgia and Arthritis

As you can see, with regular daily meditation you can change your life, your relationships, health, mind and body. You will become healthier, smarter, energized and the chances to get dangerous diseases are lowered.

Mindful Meditation in 7 Steps

Mindful meditation is research-based, western and non-sectarian meditation that exists from 2500 years ago practiced by Buddhists and was called Insight Meditation or Vipassana. It is a meditation that is especially designed to develop the skill of awareness with patience, acceptance and compassion.

Mindfulness has always been part of a human being, which means everyone has it. However, usually they haven't been advised that they possess it, that it can be cultivated and how valuable it is. The goal of the mindfulness meditation is to not to think, but to be aware of what you are thinking, and also to be aware of other ways you experience the world, like tasting, hearing, feeling, smelling through the body.

In mindfulness meditation you will try to achieve a mind that is calm and stable. What you will begin to discover is the harmony or calmness in the natural aspect of your mind. So, because you already have mindfulness in you, you just need to strengthen it and to awaken it and soon you will be able to be peaceful in your mind without any difficulties. Your mind will feel content naturally.

An important point is that when you are in the mindful state, there is intelligence. You are not blacking out. Usually people think that those who are in deep meditation don't know what is happening around them. They think that they are asleep. In fact, if you are in a meditative state where you are denying senses and their function, then you are deeply aware of the surroundings.

Design your environment

There are few certain conditions that can help you practice mindfulness. One of them is to design your own right environment because it will be easier to practice.

It is better if the space where you are planning to meditate has the feeling of sacredness and divinity, even if it is a really small space. Also, the place shouldn't be disturbing and noisy, and you shouldn't be in a situation where you can be easily distracted and provoked by jealousy, anger or any other emotions. If you are irritated or disturbed, then your practice will be affected. You could preferably wear a garment specially used only for this practice. If you practice mindfulness with this garment every day, after some time just wearing this garment will bring you into a state of mindfulness. But do not use this garment for anything else other than to meditate.

Starting Your Practice

You should meditate more frequently, but for shorter periods, like 10, 15 or 20 minutes. Don't force your mind too much, and training your mind is simple and easy. This is even good for those that really don't have time to meditate for 20 minutes at a stretch. So, it is a lot better to meditate for 10 minutes in the morning and 10 minutes in the evening. This short time is when you really work with your mind. Then after the practice simple stop and just continue with your day.

Usually you can just plop yourself to meditate and you let your mind take you wherever it wants. You have to create your own sense of discipline. So when you sit down to meditate you will remind yourself that you are here to work on your mind and to train it. It is really ok to tell these kind of things to yourself because this is a way to be inspired and motivated and to continue.

Posture

When it comes to the right posture there is one approach that Buddhist approach, the body and the mind are connected. The energy will flow better when your body is straight and erect. When it is bent, the energy flow changes and it will directly affect the process of your thoughts. The posture really affects your mind. Your physiology impacts your psychology.

If you want to use a chair to meditate, you have to sit upright with your feet touching the ground. But, if you prefer using a cushion or a mat you have to find a comfortable position, with the legs crossed and your hands should be in a position so that the palms are facing down resting on the thighs. Your hips shouldn't lean forward; your back should be erect. Once you are in this position, you will have a feeling of strength and stability.

Once you sit down the first thing that you have to do is to inhabit your body, which means to have a real sense of your body. Sometimes some people pretend that they are practicing, they can't feel their body and they can't feel it where it is. So, you have to be right there. So when you start with your mindful meditation you should spend a few minutes to settle into your posture. You will start to feel that the spine is pulled up from your head, which means the posture is straight, and that is when you settle.

So, the basic thing is to keep the upright posture. You should be in a solid situation; the shoulders will be leveled, the hips too and your spine is upright. Try to visualize how you are putting your bones in order and how they let the flash to hang off from them. This posture is used to remain awake and relaxed. The practice you are going to do is precise; you have to stay awake even though you are calm. You have to check the posture if you start to feel sleepy, and if you are getting hazy or dull.

Gazing

Meditation is the best way to develop mindfulness and because of that you have to follow strict practice, it is not difficult, just strict. So, the gaze will have to be downward, the focus needs to be two inches from your nose. Your eyes should be open, but you shouldn't stare; the gaze has to be soft. This part of the meditation is to try to reduce the sensory input as much as you can. You might start asking now, "What about sensing the environment?" Right now that is not part of the practice. You will be trying to work with your mind and to raise the gaze higher. This means you will be more districted. It is like if you had light above your head and it is shining in the room, but suddenly you are focusing down in front of you. With this you are ignoring the surroundings on purpose.

Breathing

When you do a mindfulness meditation you are becoming more familiar with your own thoughts and you are starting to recognize the movements of your mind, which you are experiencing as thoughts. You will be doing this by using an object for your meditation, which will provide a counterpoint or contrast to what is actually happening in your mind. So, when your mind wanders off and you start to think something, the awareness of that object will help in bringing you back. You can get any object in front of you to help you focus, but breathing is the best object to use when you are practicing mindfulness meditation. This is because you are focusing on the breath, which is created by your own body, and you can follow it where ever you are taking it. Moreover With the breath you are staying connected with your body and mind in the here and now.

As your meditation practice has started you will soon start to sense your body and you will sense where you are, then you will sense your breath. The entire feeling of the breath is important. You must breath naturally and you shouldn't force it. You are breathing in and out and so on. With each breath you take you become more relaxed and focused.

Thoughts

It can happen to everyone and also to you, especially if you are you starting meditation for the first time. The thoughts will be everywhere. However, any thought that will come you have to say to yourself that you understand that this specific thought is important and you will address to it later, now you are practicing your meditation. It is about how true you are to yourself and honest, during your each session.

You must understand that the mind can go wild and your thoughts will start coming up in your meditation, but you have to stay unbiased and not to take anything too personal. You can't push yourself. Don't try to be concept-free because that will never happen, even to the most experienced mindful people.

So in the labeling process, you are going to see your own discursiveness. You will notice that you have been lost in your thought and you are labeling it as "thinking". Do that without judgment and do it gently. Then come back to your breath. When you have a thought remember, no matter how bizarre or wild it may be, you just let it go and get back to your breath, go back here and now.

Each meditation that you are going to do is the journey without end along the way you will understand and discover the basic reality of who you are. In the beginning of your meditation practice the important lesson is to see the real speed of your mind. But, the tradition of meditation says that your mind doesn't have to be that way, you just have to work with it.

Release the Tension

The next step for practicing meditation is to release your tension from the body. Once you are done with the first 5 steps of mindful meditation you are aware of the body and now you can sense everything that is happening inside and also outside. So, you can also feel the tension, stress and the pain that is inside your body. All of them have been gathering inside for a long time and your body had suffered too much, but your mind was never there to help in releasing it. So, it is important to know how to release that tension inside your body.

In the position that you have chosen to do your meditation it is always easy and possible to release your tension. Once you recognize what is your tension about, it is time to be focused on it and be aware of it and with mindful breathing to release the tension from your body.

After some time, mindfulness meditation will become your habit and you will practice it with ease without having any problems in releasing any kind of emotions. Only you will understand that you are mindful and then you can take your practice to the next level. You will even be able to practice meditation when you are driving. For example, when you are in a hurry and you want to arrive to your destination fast, you will sense that your tension is starting to build up. Imagine, on top of all that you are missing the green light and you stop at the red light. Now your tension is even worse. But, use this red light as a reminder that you can release your tension in just 10 second of mindful breathing. Use the opportunity of the red light to release all the tension into your body and calm yourself down and to be back in the moment.

Walking Meditation

This seventh step of mindful meditation is not focused on a passive meditation, but in an active one. Even that this step is not connected to the other 6 is still part of mindful meditation because you already know how to be aware of your mind and body. So now by using the mindful breathing you can actually practice meditation when you are walking.

When you are practicing mindful breathing you are allowing the breath to take the place and you are aware of it and you are enjoying it. The same thing goes for mindful walking. You will be enjoying every step you take. Every step will help you to touch the incredible wonders of life. Every step will be joy.

There will be no need for you to put effort in mindful walking because you will be enjoying it. Your mind and body are connected and you are really there. You are truly alive, present and aware of the present, of here and now. With each step you are touching the wonder in you and all around you. By walking like that, every step will heal you. You will be filled with joy and peace because each step is truly miracle.

The true miracle is not to walk on water or fire or to fly. The true miracle is to be walking on Earth and you will be able to perform many miracles all the time and any time. Just place your mind at home – your body and be alive, perform this miracle, to walk on Earth.

## Chapter 11: The Signs Your Body Sends You: Strict Diets And Common Conditions

Dieting has been an integral part of people's quest on how to lose those extra pounds they have gained. Counting how many calories each food you eat has, keeping notes of everything that goes into your mouth, and choosing to follow a strict diet almost always has the exact opposite effect of losing and maintaining the lost weight on a long-term scale. Dieting and eating healthy are opposite.

Many people choose to follow diets, they do so because they actually work but in the short term. They are most appropriate for people who have reached completely unhealthy levels of weight, and those people need to lose a certain percentage of fat in order to avoid any possible fatal danger and when the dieting is over to start eating healthy and maintain a healthy lifestyle.

The good news is that according to studies, fewer and fewer people follow diets and start eating healthy instead, mainly because they have learned their lessons from mistakes of the past. People all over the world have started to understand that if your plan to lose weight does not seem possible to maintain for long, then you shouldn't even bother starting in the first place.

But how would you know if your diet is bad for you? By learning to listen to your body and the signs it sends you whenever your diet is wrong and it needs to be changed immediately. Those signs vary from subtle to downright obvious, but they will always be there since the plan of your diet will influence your body on a much bigger scale than you could ever imagine. What we place inside our bodies will affect your skin, your mind, and how productive you are during the day. There are not a few cases of people whose diet and their body shows them that their diet is not appropriate for their health. Let us see all those signs that your body tells you to stop this dietary plan and start eating healthy.

One sign of bad dietary plans is bad breath caused by Ketosis, the result of metabolic process that happens when glucose, a source of energy, is not enough in our bodies and our metabolism burns fat. This results in creating acids named "ketones" that can make your breath smell bad. People who follow low carb diets are more prone to accumulate ketones to their breath and these diets and ketones can be extremely dangerous for people that have type 1 diabetes. They should visit a doctor due to the fact that ketones may mean that there is not enough insulin in their bodies. The problem will be resolved if you increase your eating portions so that the required energy you need is taken through food. On the other hand, bad breath can be caused also from smoking, coffee, and by not caring for your teeth enough.

If your hair is thinning it means that your iron levels are low. Iron is essential to the production of red blood cells and they in turn transfer oxygen throughout our blood. If your iron levels are low, you may feel sluggish and your hair will get thinner. Eating green vegetables such as broccoli and spinach, and red meat will enhance your iron levels. For women, iron levels could fall even further due to menstruation and not only due to bad diet programs, so they should follow a dietary plan which is full in iron.

If you notice that you suffer from continual diarrhea, you may have Coeliac disease. Coeliac disease is a reaction of our immune system from eating gluten found in barley, wheat, and rye. Our small intestine is triggered by eating gluten and can lead to weight loss, abdominal pain, and diarrhea. If you cut off gluten from your dietary plan, the problem will be resolved and keep in mind that Coeliac disease is completely different from gluten intolerance even though they have the same symptoms.

If you feel constipated, it is your body's way of telling you that you are not drinking enough water and your diet is lacking in fiber. For regular and normal bowel movement, both water and fiber are needed since the fiber is able to attract water which in turn transfers it in the body in an easier way. In such cases, drink more water and at the same time add to your diet high fiber foods, like whole grains, nuts, beans, and dried fruit.

If you feel constantly tired and that your energy levels are low, there is a high chance that you are taking into your body too much sugar. Too much sugar or other carbohydrates can make you feel tired all the time and for you to have low energy levels. This happens because the sugar will raise the insulin that is in your body at first, but if you have a daily intake of more sugar than necessary; it will cause your energy levels to fall. Don't make the mistake of believing that when you feel less energetic it is right to eat more sugar. On the contrary, reduce your sugar and your energy will elevate and stabilize in no time.

If you are going to the toilet frequently to release fluid, you are dehydrated. Often people think the opposite is true, but even if when you drink too much water, your bladder is full and triggers the brain signaling you that it is time to relieve yourself, this is not always the case. Your bladder may also be irritated by your urine is concentrated in one specific location. The solution to this problem is to drink much more water in order for your urine to be clearer than yellow.

If you constantly feel as if you are swollen all the time, this is a sure sign of your following a bad diet plan. If you feel gassy, especially after eating dairy products, you might even be lactose intolerant. There are signs that will tell you if you suffer from this condition such as nausea, vomiting, gas, diarrhea and cramps in the abdomen area that will begin from thirty minutes to two hours after eating anything that contains lactose. Lactose intolerance is happening due to the fact that lactase, an enzyme that is produced in our small intestine, is insufficient in our bodies.

Even though many people exist, whose lactase levels are low and have no problems in digesting dairy products without any problems, there are also those who face the mentioned symptoms after they eat dairy foods. In this case, the lactose contained in the food you eat is directly transferred into the colon without first being processed and absorbed. When it reaches the colon, undigested lactose is coming in contact with normal bacteria, resulting in the signs of lactose intolerance.

When you are always hungry at the end of the day by following a specific diet, then you are not following the right diet for you and your body suffers along with you.

After a day of successfully following your diet plan, night time is another matter. You may be so hungry that even your willpower is not strong enough to keep you from a bag of chips. Eating excessively is caused by your body's demand that it doesn't get all the necessary nutrients needed to be full and healthy. Keep in mind that a proper diet with the purpose of being healthy and right for people, should not eliminate food groups unless it is necessary for medical reasons.

A psychological sign of you following the wrong diet plan is if you are constantly in a bad mood. Food cravings will irritate you when you are trying to cut down your carbs and calories. Also, the sugar in your blood is low during this process, a fact that contributes to severe mood swings.

Research has shown that diets consisting of low carb consumption can have a severe effect on your thyroid, which is responsible for the temperature of your body. If your thyroid slows down, you will feel cold even during summer. Try not to cut down all carbs. Just make certain that you include in your diet complex carbs such as whole grain bread, and more other foods like pasta.

Another sure sign of an unhealthy diet is wrinkles and acne. Diets that are lacking vitamin A will have a huge impact on your skin since vitamin A has an essential role in controlling the production of retinoid. Any deficiency caused to this nutrient could also drive you to have brittle nails and dry hair. To solve this problem, eat foods that are rich in vitamin A such as carrots or sweet potatoes.

Mental illnesses may stem from a bad and unbalanced diet. If you feel depressed all the time, you may follow a diet that is not providing you enough minerals, vitamins and Omega-3 acids. Your mood can be changed by taking nutritional supplements with vitamin B12. They are usually prescribed to patients that are trying to tackle mental illnesses.

Memory can also be affected by eating badly. According to researches, saturated fats had an effect on women who showed lower memory abilities and were slower on thinking tests when compared to those women that did not eat those saturated fats. If you want a sharp memory, you should do well to avoid fast food and French fries.

Our immune system is also affected by a bad diet. For example, you may always be sick if you follow a low-protein diet since proteins help you by reinforcing your immune system. If you ban essential nutrients of your body, you will weaken your immune system and therefore you will leave yourself open to illnesses. Make sure to stay healthy and eat many proteins such as lean meats, and beans.

When you have a small cut or even a larger injury, you may have noticed that it takes more time to heal than the time it takes on other people. For a wound to heal fast and appropriately, it requires a considerable amount of nutrients to be in your body, so if you heal slowly it may be due to the fact that your nutrients are not enough to help through the process. A bad diet can and will affect the resilience of the new tissue, the time you will need to recover from a wound, no matter how small it is, as well as how effectively your body will battle an infection that may affect the wound. Research has shown that proper amounts of protein, nutrients, and calories are needed for wounds to be healed effectively.

The above are signs of the physical kind your body is showing you to indicate that something is really wrong with your diet and your overall health. However, our body includes our mind and hence the emotional responses to a bad lifestyle. We mentioned how depression can be enhanced by strict diets and generally following a bad lifestyle. This can also happen when it comes to anxiety. Although your way of eating is not scientifically proven that can cause an anxiety disorder, it may make the symptoms of anxiety worse. Strict diets for weight loss may lead you to anxious moods as well as restricting calories along with proteins. Also, overeating will cause the same effects because it will lead to weight gain. Eating too little or too much will increase your anxiety due to the fact that you will never be satisfied with the ending result. A balanced diet will resolve this problem since you will see the desired results in your body as well as in your emotional responses.

Anxiety disorder can be revealed through physical symptoms that will warn you of the condition. There are many types of anxiety disorders such as panic disorders, separation anxiety, generalized anxiety disorder, phobias, social anxiety, and obsessive-compulsive disorder that have unique symptoms linked to fears that each type of anxiety can produce. Generally, anxiety disorders have many common physical symptoms and your body will express them to warn you of the danger.

These signs include nausea, stomach pains, digestive trouble, tiredness and fatigue, sleep issues such as insomnia, headaches, shortness of breath or rapid breathing, sweating, increased heart rate, muscle pain or tension, shaking or trembling. For example, if you are going through a panic attack you may feel dizzy, develop chest pain, have trouble breathing, and feel as if you are choking, or feel as though you may pass out.

Keep in mind that anxiety is how the body responds to stress and alerts you to potential threats that you should be prepared to deal with. For example, you may breathe faster due to the fact that your lungs are trying to take in more oxygen just in case the need arises to escape from a situation.

Stress can also be caused by bad eating habits. People who follow a strict diet are more prone to develop emotional stress than those who follow a balanced diet. Fewer calories and carbohydrates are likely to multiply stress since both are essential for the brain to work correctly as well as to produce a number of chemicals that make people feel good, like serotonin. However, eating more food than is necessary for our bodies can also enhance stress because we gain weight and therefore we may get depressed by our image and stress out to lose this extra weight by following strict and unbalanced diets.

What happens when we suffer from depression? What are the physical symptoms that warn us of this disorder? Most people are aware of the emotional symptoms, but our bodies react to depression too so as to warn us of the dangers we are placing ourselves into. Depression causes constant and persistent emotions of sadness and a lack of interest in things about your life that you previously loved. This is the main reason why depression is a dangerous mood disorder since it can lead you to think that life is not worth living anymore.

The physical symptoms of depression include back pain and headaches that if they existed before as migraines they will probably get worse. Also, you will endure chest pain, but it may also occur due to a serious lung, heart, stomach condition. You may also have diarrhea or be constipated for long periods of time. Added to this, you will feel tired as if getting out of bed is an impossible task, no matter how much sleep you get.

However, people who suffer from depression, are not able to sleep as well as they did before. They may not even be able to fall asleep once they retire for the night or wake up too early while other people may sleep much more than they normally did, before developing depression. Last but not least, depressed people will notice a change in their appetite which will result in either losing weight or gain weight. The result is different for every person.

The above are some of the signs our bodies will show us when we follow a bad diet, when we have lactose intolerance, when we have anxiety or when we suffer from depression. What happens though, when our body has to warn us that our overall health? How will your body tell you that you need to make different lifestyle choices and take care of it more? There are signs that will show you when the time has come to take responsibility for your body and start listening to it.

Your skin will show you if you take care of your health appropriately. With the exception of people who are diagnosed with skin issues such as acne, bad skin will tell the tale of your overall state of health. If you keep seeing blemishes or stretch marks, it can be the result of a bad diet or lack of a daily skincare routine and cleanliness.

Sleep is extremely important for following a healthy lifestyle and if you are not able to sleep at night, there can be many reasons for this occurrence such as getting less caffeine, following a bad dietary plan, and not letting out much energy during the day that prevents you from falling asleep. Eight hours of sleep a day is required for us to stay healthy and productive throughout our lives. Pinpoint the problems that are causing your body to refuse to get the rest it needs and make the necessary changes.

Low vitamin levels can be expressed through constantly chapped lips, bad fingernails and toenails or skin problems. If you have to always apply lip balm in order for your lips to seem healthy, then you need a vitamin boost. Make the necessary changes to your diet and when you get the appropriate nutrients, you will notice your lips improving too. Usually, chapped lips indicate a deficiency of vitamin B-2 or else riboflavin. This vitamin is necessary for healthy nails, skin, and hair. You can get vitamin B-2 by eating dairy products, vegetables, eggs, nuts, beans, and lean meats. Adult males need 1.3 milligrams of vitamin B-2 while adult females need 1.0 milligrams of vitamin B-2 in their system.

Another vitamin your body needs and when not found in appropriate numbers in your system may cause chapped lips, skin problems or swollen tongue is vitamin B-3 or else niacin. To receive the needed amount of 13 to 20 milligrams of vitamin B-3 per day, you need to eat foods such as beef, poultry, tune, been, milk, vegetables, and halibut. An insufficient amount of vitamin B-6 or else pyridoxine can also be a sign of skin problems and cracks found at the corners of your mouth. Adult women and men up to 50 years of age should receive 1.3 milligrams of vitamin B-6 every day from food such as legumes, meats, green vegetables, and whole grains.

Another physical sign your body shows that you are not healthy is cold feet and hands. Even though the environment you live in may be the cause, if you constantly feel that your hands and feet are cold, it may be considered as a sign of cardiovascular problems, specifically circulation issues. In other words, there is not enough blood flowing in certain places in your body.

Another sign you should watch out for is if you have noticed that you are getting shorter. As we age, it is normal to lose our height, but when this is happening earlier than is considered normal and in extremely small amounts, it can be a sign of a serious health problem such as bone loss. Another condition that can be attributed to this situation is not receiving enough essential nutrients such as calcium and protein. In the long term, this condition may lead to loss of the density of the bones and fractures.

When your legs swell, it may be a way of your body saying that there may be a problem with your kidney, heart or thyroid condition Thyroid problems are also indicated through your neck swelling and specifically, your thyroid may be overactive when your neck swelling happens out of the blue and at an extreme speed.

For women, dark and coarse hairs that grow on the chin may be a sign of polycystic ovary syndrome. There is a hormonal anomaly that can also affect a woman's period and thus a woman's fertility. Other signs of polycystic ovary syndrome are skin issues from enhanced levels of androgens, irregular period, weight gain at the area around the stomach, trouble sleeping, depression and/or anxiety, and ovarian cysts.

Also, if your big toe looks swollen and you haven't injured it in any way, it could be a sign and an early symptom of gout. Gout is extremely painful and can place you at the risk of developing chronic diseases such as kidney disease and elevated blood pressure. Another sign of gout is swollen joints, so if you notice these two symptoms happening for prolonged periods of time, a visit to your doctor is necessary.

When you wake up and you still feel exhausted, it may be a physical sign of restless leg syndrome, in other words, we wake up still feeling tired because our bodies never truly entered a relaxed state during the night. You may also have noticed an urge of moving your legs, especially when you sit down. A visit to your doctor will surely be a good move since he or she will point you in the right direction.

If you notice that you are sweating through your clothes and specifically on your underarms, face, or hands, you may have hyperhidrosis. It can be a sign of a medical condition, for example, an overactive thyroid, even though the sweat is harmless. If you also experience weight loss, fever, or shortness in your breath, you should visit your doctor due to the fact that there are several medical reasons for your excess sweating such as lung or heart disease. You should start immediately by changing your diet and cut back on spicy food, curries, and garlic.

Also, if you notice skin tags appearing in high numbers, it could be a sign of type 2 diabetes. They are caused by insulin-like growth factor 1 that is a protein commonly found in diabetes and can arouse skin overgrowth. If you also notice yellow bumps on your glutes, feet, joints, and hands it may be a warning of fat concentration under your skin. These spots are called xanthomas and are a warning that your blood fats such as cholesterol are extremely high. Another condition they can indicate is diabetes, some types of cancers, and pancreatitis.

Last but not least, snoring is a common sign of sleep apnea that is linked with an increased risk of heart disease. Snoring is also linked to thickening carotid arteries in the neck and such damage can lead to heart attack and stroke. Studies have shown that snoring is found more commonly to people that smoke, have high cholesterol or are overweight.

If you push yourself and overdo it with your body, you might end up exhausted and do more harm to your body than good. If you don't listen to what your body has to say, how will you know what it needs and what should you do in order for you to live a healthy and long life? Don't be fooled by today's world. You may be busy and postpone your visit to the doctor since you think any symptom your body shows, will pass. You don't care about following a healthy and balanced diet because straining your body will get you the desired results faster, so how you look is the only thing that matters.

Keep in mind that your body will help you and be there for you if you take care of it. Your body is the house of your soul and it needs to be cared for as you take care of the house you live in. If your body thrives, you will thrive. If your body is healthy, you will be healthy. When we visit the doctor, we do so because we saw something. We noticed something was not going well within our body. So, how could you start forging this bond with your body? How can you start listening to it?

## Chapter 12: Steps To Mindfulness

This list of the best hotels in Singapore has been handpicked by our very own team of hotel experts. Singapore is known worldwide for its excellent shopping choices, fine dining, lifestyle and quality accommodation choices. It's hard to imagine a trip to this fabulous place without making the best of the wide range of hotels in the city-state and really making sure that your choice complements your stay.

So browse through our Top 10 Singapore Hotels and decide for yourself where you'll stay when visiting this vibrant and colourful destination. You can click on each one to see it up in detail, as well as check some of the best live rates for each one online.

First Mindfulness Exercise: Mindful Breathing

The first exercise is very simple, but the power, the result, can be very great. The exercise is simply to identify the in-breath as in-breath and the out-breath as out-breath. When you breathe in, you know that this is your in-breath. When you breathe out, you are mindful that this is your out-breath.

Just recognize: this is an in-breath, this is an out-breath. Very simple, very easy. In order to recognize your in-breath as in-breath, you have to bring your mind home to yourself. What is recognizing your in-breath is your mind, and the object of your mind—the object of your mindfulness—is the in-breath. Mindfulness is always mindful of something. When you drink your tea mindfully, it's called mindfulness of drinking. When you walk mindfully, it's called mindfulness of walking. And when you breathe mindfully, that is mindfulness of breathing.

So the object of your mindfulness is your breath, and you just focus your attention on it. Breathing in, this is my in-breath. Breathing out, this is my out-breath. When you do that, the mental discourse will stop. You don't think anymore. You don't have to make an effort to stop your thinking; you bring your attention to your in-breath and the mental discourse just stops. That is the miracle of the practice. You don't think of the past anymore. You don't think of the future. You don't think of your projects, because you are focusing your attention, your mindfulness, on your breath.

Second Mindfulness Exercise: Concentration

The second exercise is that while you breathe in, you follow your in-breath from the beginning to the end. If your in-breath lasts three or four seconds, then your mindfulness also lasts three or four seconds. Breathing in, I follow my in-breath all the way through. Breathing out, I follow my out-breath all the way through. From the beginning of my out-breath to the end of my out-breath, my mind is **always** with it. Therefore, mindfulness becomes uninterrupted, and the quality of your concentration is improved.

So the second exercise is to follow your in-breath and your out-breath all the way through. Whether they are short or long, it doesn't matter. What is important is that you follow your in-breath from the beginning to the end. Your awareness is sustained. There is no interruption. Suppose you are breathing in, and then you think, "Oh, I forgot to turn off the light in my room." There is an interruption. Just stick to your in-breath all the way through. Then you cultivate your mindfulness and your concentration. You become your in-breath. You become your out-breath. If you continue like that, your breathing will naturally become deeper and slower, more harmonious and peaceful. You don't have to make any effort—it happens naturally.

Third Mindfulness Exercise: Awareness of Your Body

The third exercise is to become aware of your body as you are breathing. "Breathing in, I am aware of my whole body." This takes it one step further.

In the first exercise, you became aware of your in-breath and your out-breath. Because you have now generated the energy of mindfulness through mindful breathing, you can use that energy to recognize your body.

"Breathing in, I am aware of my body. Breathing out, I am aware of my body." I know my body is **there**. This brings the mind wholly back to the body. Mind and body become one reality. When your mind is with your body, you are well-established in the here and the now. You are fully alive. You can be in touch with the wonders of life that are available in yourself and around you.

This exercise is simple, but the effect of the oneness of body and mind is very great. In our daily lives, we are seldom in that situation. Our body is there but our mind is elsewhere. Our mind may be caught in the past or in the future, in regrets, sorrow, fear, or uncertainty, and so our mind is not there. Someone may be present in the house, but he's not really there, his mind is not there. His mind is with the future, with his projects, and he's not there for his children or his spouse. Maybe you could say to him, "Anybody home?" and help him bring his mind back to his body.

So the third exercise is to become aware of your body. "Breathing in, I'm aware of my body." When you practice mindful breathing, the quality of your in-breath and out-breath will be improved. There is more peace and harmony in your breathing, and if you continue to practice like that, the peace and the harmony will penetrate into the body, and the body will profit.

Fourth Mindfulness Exercise: Releasing Tension

The next exercise is to release the tension in the body. When you are truly aware of your body, you notice there is some tension and pain in your body, some stress. The tension and pain have been accumulating for a long time and our bodies suffer, but our mind is not there to help release it. Therefore, it is very important to learn how to release the tension in the body.

In a sitting, lying, or standing position, it's always possible to release the tension. You can practice total relaxation, deep relaxation, in a sitting or lying position. While you are driving your car, you might notice the tension in your body. You are eager to arrive and you don't enjoy the time you spend driving. When you come to a red light, you are eager for the red light to become a green light so that you can continue. But the red light can be a signal. It can be a reminder that there is tension in you, the stress of wanting to arrive as quickly as possible. If you recognize that, you can make use of the red light. You can sit back and relax—take the ten seconds the light is red to practice mindful breathing and release the tension in the body.

So next time you're stopped at a red light, you might like to sit back and practice the fourth exercise: "Breathing in, I'm aware of my body. Breathing out, I release the tension in my body." Peace is possible at that moment, and it can be practiced many times a day—in the workplace, while you are driving, while you are cooking, while you are doing the dishes, while you are watering the vegetable garden. It is always possible to practice releasing the tension in yourself.

Walking Meditation

When you practice mindful breathing you simply allow your in breath to take place. You become aware of it and enjoy it. Effortlessness. The same thing is true with mindful walking. Every step is enjoyable.

Every step helps you touch the wonders of life. Every step is joy. That is possible.

You don't have to make any effort during walking meditation, because it is enjoyable. You are there, body and mind together. You are fully alive, fully present in the here and the now. With every step, you touch the wonders of life that are in you and around you. When you walk like that, every step brings healing. Every step brings peace and joy, because every step is a miracle.

The real miracle is not to fly or walk on fire. The real miracle is to walk on the Earth, and you can perform that miracle at any time. Just bring your mind home to your body, become alive, and perform the miracle of walking on Earth.

## Chapter 13: Living In The Moment

This is the whole point of mindfulness — to experience life as it happens, not getting stuck in some dream world and having to face nasty consequences for your inattention. A person who lives in the moment has the best chances of being fulfilled and achieving their goals because they can exploit their potential to the last drain. When you live in the moment, it means that you're in touch with your thoughts, feelings, and body sensations. Although living in the moment might sound like a basic thing, most people are nowhere close to that. Our thoughts, worries, regrets, fears, and every other imaginable type of negative energy have held us back from living in the moment. Mindfulness is a great mental training that helps people become the best version of themselves by empowering them to be aware of their reality. The following are some of the tips for living in the moment.

Start small

If you have been living a disorganized life, staggering from one scene of confusion to the next, it is nearly impossible to suddenly start living in the moment. You have to take baby steps into this thing. You must first identify one or two areas that you need to work on and then slowly apply the effort. If it is meditation, start at three minutes and then increase the time limits as you grow into the practice.

Notice sensory details about routine activities

There are various things that are part of our routine that we never pay a thought. We go through these activities like mindless zombies which shouldn't be the case. For instance, when you are brushing your teeth in the morning, take a moment to savor the taste and fragrance of your toothpaste. Paying attention to the small things increases your capacity to notice the big ones as well.

Redirect your mind

Meditation is one of the exercises central to mindfulness. The main aim of meditation is to clear away the noise from your mind and achieve a state of peaceful existence. But whenever we practice meditation, we find our minds wandering off. In such instances, we shouldn't be hard on ourselves, but rather we should gently redirect our thoughts back into the thought that we had been focusing on.

The power of mindfulness cues

Most people want to practice mindfulness and it's one of the things that they have given thought to and made a mental note of trying it out. However, the complexities of life get in the way and mindfulness becomes a distant thought. In order to protect yourself against such an issue, you might consider keeping a mindfulness cue. This is basically an item that will constantly remind you of mindfulness. For instance, you may wear a band or necklace with the inscription "mindfulness" so that every time you look at it you're reminded of practicing mindfulness.

Smile and laugh

Your circumstances are not too bleak that you cannot afford to smile or laugh. Men march into wars and as the fight progresses — they have something to laugh about. Think about it. Nothing could be more gruesome than having your friends falling to their deaths around you from enemy attacks and yet these people are known to have a joyous spirit to them. No matter what nightmares you are trapped in, you must learn to have a sense of humor.

Gratitude

One of the things responsible for taking our focus away is the lust that we have for more acquisitions. We might have a store of riches but it is never enough and we are ready to kill for more. This mindset of lust blinds us to our blessings. If we'd take a moment to appreciate the things that are right about our lives, we'd be a lot less greedy. Gratefulness not only stops the cycle of negativity but also empowers a person to take notice of their reality at an even deeper level.

Breathing

No other exercise is as potent as breathing when it comes to eliminating clutter from our minds. And when we rid ourselves of mental clutter, we free ourselves up and are much more capable of experiencing our reality. And breathing has a host of other benefits that ensure your holistic development.

**Forgiveness**

Each one of us carries some baggage from the past. We ran into people that did us dirty and we have nothing but hatred for them. But holding on to such grudges takes our power away. We ought to forgive and free ourselves of the emotional burden of grudges. And this will help us savor our present moment even much more deeply.

Limit social media use

Social media is purposely aimed to call to the narcissistic monster buried inside us. Forget the rationality — every person on social media is trying to get some attention. But there's nothing with that except there's a problem when social media goes from harmless fun into a time black hole. Cut back the time you spend updating your Facebook or Instagram and stalking both your friends and enemies. Now, you have more energy to perceive your thoughts, emotions, and reality.

Get rid of your unworthy belongings

Get rid of your worthless possessions. They will free up space and reinforce positive energy. If it is clothes that no longer fit you, give them away to a charity. If it's car that's slowly rotting away in your backyard, sell it off. Getting rid of worthless possessions will not only improve your moods and make you more energetic but might also have a monetary benefit.

Learn to move on

When people think of moving on, they approach it from the perspective of moving on from failure alone. Wrong! You should learn to move on from both your successes and failures. If you're so much taken with your success, you won't have the discipline to work on other important stuff and this could bring about stagnation. But if there's a sense of moving, an urgency to your life, you are more likely to stay grounded and realistic.

**Chapter 14: Living In The Moment**

This is the whole point of mindfulness — to experience life as it happens, not getting stuck in some dream world and having to face nasty consequences for your inattention. A person who lives in the moment has the best chances of being fulfilled and achieving their goals because they can exploit their potential to the last drain. When you live in the moment, it means that you're in touch with your thoughts, feelings, and body sensations. Although living in the moment might sound like a basic thing, most people are nowhere close to that. Our thoughts, worries, regrets, fears, and every other imaginable type of negative energy have held us back from living in the moment. Mindfulness is a great mental training that helps people become the best version of themselves by empowering them to be aware of their reality. The following are some of the tips for living in the moment.

Start small

If you have been living a disorganized life, staggering from one scene of confusion to the next, it is nearly impossible to suddenly start living in the moment. You have to take baby steps into this thing. You must first identify one or two areas that you need to work on and then slowly apply the effort. If it is meditation, start at three minutes and then increase the time limits as you grow into the practice.

Notice sensory details about routine activities

There are various things that are part of our routine that we never pay a thought. We go through these activities like mindless zombies which shouldn't be the case. For instance, when you are brushing your teeth in the morning, take a moment to savor the taste and fragrance of your toothpaste. Paying attention to the small things increases your capacity to notice the big ones as well.

Redirect your mind

Meditation is one of the exercises central to mindfulness. The main aim of meditation is to clear away the noise from your mind and achieve a state of peaceful existence. But whenever we practice meditation, we find our minds wandering off. In such instances, we shouldn't be hard on ourselves, but rather we should gently redirect our thoughts back into the thought that we had been focusing on.

The power of mindfulness cues

Most people want to practice mindfulness and it's one of the things that they have given thought to and made a mental note of trying it out. However, the complexities of life get in the way and mindfulness becomes a distant thought. In order to protect yourself against such an issue, you might consider keeping a mindfulness cue. This is basically an item that will constantly remind you of mindfulness. For instance, you may wear a band or necklace with the inscription "mindfulness" so that every time you look at it you're reminded of practicing mindfulness.

Smile and laugh

Your circumstances are not too bleak that you cannot afford to smile or laugh. Men march into wars and as the fight progresses —they have something to laugh about. Think about it. Nothing could be more gruesome than having your friends falling to their deaths around you from enemy attacks and yet these people are known to have a joyous spirit to them. No matter what nightmares you are trapped in, you must learn to have a sense of humor.

Gratitude

One of the things responsible for taking our focus away is the lust that we have for more acquisitions. We might have a store of riches but it is never enough and we are ready to kill for more. This mindset of lust blinds us to our blessings. If we'd take a moment to appreciate the things that are right about our lives, we'd be a lot less greedy. Gratefulness not only stops the cycle of negativity but also empowers a person to take notice of their reality at an even deeper level.

Breathing

No other exercise is as potent as breathing when it comes to eliminating clutter from our minds. And when we rid ourselves of mental clutter, we free ourselves up and are much more capable of experiencing our reality. And breathing has a host of other benefits that ensure your holistic development.

Forgiveness

Each one of us carries some baggage from the past. We ran into people that did us dirty and we have nothing but hatred for them. But holding on to such grudges takes our power away. We ought to forgive and free ourselves of the emotional burden of grudges. And this will help us savor our present moment even much more deeply.

Limit social media use

Social media is purposely aimed to call to the narcissistic monster buried inside us. Forget the rationality — every person on social media is trying to get some attention. But there's nothing with that except there's a problem when social media goes from harmless fun into a time black hole. Cut back the time you spend updating your Facebook or Instagram and stalking both your friends and enemies. Now, you have more energy to perceive your thoughts, emotions, and reality.

Get rid of your unworthy belongings

Get rid of your worthless possessions. They will free up space and reinforce positive energy. If it is clothes that no longer fit you, give them away to a charity. If it's car that's slowly rotting away in your backyard, sell it off. Getting rid of worthless possessions will not only improve your moods and make you more energetic but might also have a monetary benefit.

Learn to move on

When people think of moving on, they approach it from the perspective of moving on from failure alone. Wrong! You should learn to move on from both your successes and failures. If you're so much taken with your success, you won't have the discipline to work on other important stuffand this could bring about stagnation. But if there's a sense of moving, an urgency to your life, you are more likely to stay grounded and realistic.

## Chapter 15: How To Stay Motivated To Do Mindfulness Meditation

By reaching this chapter, it is safe to assume that you have gained deeper appreciation for mindfulness and a desire to make meditation a part of your daily routine. Now the question is, how do you maintain this zeal?

In other words, how do you stay motivated to meditate no matter how "busy" today's agenda is? Here, you can find the strategies to keep you motivated to meditate for the rest of your life.

Identify the Obstacles

To create a solution to any problem, the first step is to identify the cause. Ask yourself, "What is keeping me from meditating today?" Respond as honestly as you can without judging yourself. Some of the most common obstacles to regular meditation are that you are "too busy," "not in the mood," or "too restless."

It is natural to avoid something that you have not yet formed into a habit, after all. The important thing here is that you can write down all the reasons your mind can come up with.

In fact, you can even use mindfulness meditation to become aware of what is keeping you from doing it regularly. Try a five or ten minute mindful breathing meditation. While doing so, acknowledge any of the thoughts that cross your mind as you meditate. After the session, take note of those thoughts and consider whether they may be obstacles.

Overcome the Obstacles

After identifying the obstacles, the next step is to make adjustments so that your mind will no longer perceive them as so. It helps create a list made up of two columns: the first column contains the obstacles, and the second holds the best solution you can come up with for each.

For example, if you think you do not have time to spend 20 minutes a day meditating, set aside 5 minutes instead.

If find yourself easily distracted whenever you meditate, schedule it in the morning right after waking up or right before going to bed at night. Most people will still be asleep or are too tired to distract you during these times.

Create a Designated "Meditation Corner"

No matter where you live or work, you can always find a quiet place where you can meditate for a few minutes each day. By creating this little space, you are more likely to retreat to it and practice mindfulness meditation. Having to constantly find a spot, on the other hand, may discourage you to make it into a habit.

A great idea is to set up a little corner in your bedroom dedicated solely for meditation. Place a cushion on it and add a few items that you feel will set the right mood to meditate.

Some like to focus on a candles light, so they keep a candle close by (just make sure that it is at a safe distance from anything that might catch fire). Some like to meditate on scents, so they light different incense in each session. Others like to sit next to a window facing a garden because looking at nature helps them relax. If they do not have the luxury of facing a garden, they will hang a calming picture on the wall.

How you design your little meditation corner is entirely up to you.

Set a Meditation "Appointment"

If you are the kind of person who likes to use a planner or a calendar to set appointments, then you can definitely time block a meditation session into your day, no matter how short. For instance, if you find that you have a spare 15 minutes between two meetings, you can use it to schedule your meditation session.

Another great way to remind yourself to meditate regularly is to set an alarm on your smartphone. That way, it will not fail to cross your mind.

Play Meditation Music

Most people love to listen to music. If you are no exception to that, then you will definitely enjoy mindfulness meditation even more if you play relaxing music in the background. You can choose from hundreds of free meditation music tracks online, starting from YouTube. Go ahead and listen to one right now.

After choosing a couple of songs that you really like, you can create a playlist to quickly play during each meditation session.

Add Variety

If you grow bored with the same old meditation routine, you definitely have full control should consider switching it up. Doing something new that will keep you challenged and even more motivated. That is just how the human mind works.

For instance, you can try walking meditation one day then sitting meditation the next. You can also try breathing mindfulness one time and eating mindfulness the next.

If you are bored with the same old meditation corner, go out there and meditate in the park or at the beach. You can even focus on the present moment as you listen to your favorite music. You can also try different mindfulness meditation apps on your smartphone, because each app comes with its own special styles.

Join a Community

In most cases, extroverted people are more likely to give up mindfulness meditation than introverts because being alone seems to deplete their energy. If you consider this to be the case for you, then the best solution is to find a group of people who share the same passion and dedication towards meditation as you do.

Search online for nearby meditation groups in your area. You can even organize one if there is none. Even weekly meetings of a mindful meditation group can really make a big difference to your routine.

Keep a Meditation Journal

Those who love to write will find that keeping a meditation journal will encourage them to meditate more often. Some of the insights you can gain from mindfulness meditation are quite profound, so it helps to reflect on them after the session. The journal can also help you create a sense of self-awareness because you will be writing your own thoughts.

Since your journal houses all the past sentiments and experiences you have had regarding mindfulness meditation, you can read back on your previous entries and watch how you have progressed.

You do not have to make your journal entries long to keep a meditation journal. You can even keep it as simple as the following example:

10/22/2016: Mindful breathing meditation for 10 minutes in my meditation corner.

Had to force self to meditate, but minutes into the session I forgot how restless I was and was able to sustain my focus. Felt relaxed and calm throughout the session.

Aside from all these tips, there are plenty of other creative ways to stay motivated. You may even discover other strategies as you continue to meditate each day. What matters is that you view mindfulness as an essential part of your life, because when you do your mind will find ways to turn meditation into a habit.

## Chapter 16: Meditation On Thoughts

Meditation on thoughts is any kind of meditation where we go the extra mile of examining the kind of thoughts that pass through our minds. We also go as far as assessing the part of the mind that creates these types of thoughts. The main aim of mindfulness meditation is to calm both your emotions and thoughts. You can be able to lower your degree of mental restlessness just by being more centered in the present. Increasing sensitive listening is one of the most effective ways of achieving this.

But first, you will have to listen to your outside world before coming to the interiors. You should start with the ones that are loudest, such as sounds in the traffic or sounds in your house. After that, you can try listening to more subtle sounds such as wind in the trees or a distant chirping bird. Once you have successfully achieved that, you should then be aware of very soft sounds, the sound of your heartbeat or the sound of your breath.

When you begin to listen to your own thoughts, all you need to do is to observe the stream of consciousness. You should also be very careful to maintain the perspective of a listener or an observer. You should not get drawn in a thought entirely that you even become lost in it. But if that occurs – and it almost surely will – just restore your attention back to the state of mindfulness. You won't believe the number of thoughts that will be vying for your own attention.

The next thing you will need to do is to get behind your thoughts and observe your feelings. As you get more still. You will realize that thoughts usually rise out of the underlying emotion: concern or anxiety, fear or hope, compassion, and love. While observing these underlying feelings, you should not go the extent of identifying with them. You should just be increasingly aware of the role of your consciousness.

You should never forget to focus your mind entirely on the present. You should let go of the past – regrets, memories, and of the tendency to think of ways you can change the situation. You should just accept what has occurred since you cannot change them, anyway. Get rid of all the thoughts of the future, and you should not allow your mind to think about the projects or plans that are in the future. All you need to do about the future is to observe the underlying feelings that come with it. However, you should get rid of the anxiety and the expectations that inevitably come with them. You should be entirely in the here and now.

As you become more interiorized with your thoughts, you will be aware of particular fundamental traits to your consciousness. You will be able to feel the deep peace that always comes with inner silence. As that happens, you will also enjoy the expansive love, which radiates out to the outside world. That will also lead you into discovering a great sense of joy, which is not dependent on any situation. You should meditate on these qualities, and you will attain something towards the end. You will feel these qualities expanding to a point where they fill all your consciousness, and chasing away the tendency of the mind to always be restless. You should then become absorbed in the inner silence.

A Meditation on Observing Thoughts, in a Non-Judgmental Way

The main aim of guided meditation is to let the thoughts come and do, so you can easily avoid getting sucked into them.

First of all, take a few moments to settle into entirely feeling your body, breathing and sitting, or breathing and lying down, flowing with the breath waves moment by moment, while taking a rest in awareness. This is a type of awareness that incorporates the entirety of the breath scape and the bodyscape, as they tend to express themselves, each passing moment. In awareness, you will witness life unfolds here and now in the body.

When you finally get ready, you should think of letting go of the body in its entirety and the breath. Enabling them to recede into the background, or even rest in the wings is still very highly present but less featured. As this happens, you should then invite the whole domain of feelings and thoughts, as well as mood states to be the center stage in the awareness field.

For a given time attending to the thought stream as opposed to being taken away by the emotional charge or content of the given thought, but instead comfortably resting on the stream of thoughts or just the bank of the thoughts, enabling the thoughts when and if they arise not only to be known and recognized, but also to be recognized and felt, as thoughts, and events in the awareness field.

The thoughts should be recognized as mental occurrences, events, and secretions of the thinking mind. They should be seen as independent of their emotional change and their content, even if the emotional charge and the content are known and seen.

You should see any and all of these thoughts just as bubbles, currents, and eddies that are within the stream, as opposed to seeing them as facts or some truth of things. You should not care about their content, their tendency to reappear, their urgency, their emotional charge, whether they are repulsive, unpleasant, seductive or just pleasant.

Expand the metaphor that states that seeing these fleeting thought events more like bubbles originating from a boiling water pot or like clouds in the sky. Or just like writing on water, arising for a short time, and lingering for the shortest of the instances, before dissolving back to the formlessness nature from where they came. You should relate to their main content as if it were of come relative relevance and importance to say the kind of meal you tool for dinner several nights ago. Do this even if a given thought is insightful and compelling.

What you need to do now is to let all the bad thoughts just come and go – both the thoughts and the sensations. You should not prefer some to others, or pursue some over others, just do it without judging. You should just rest in an awareness of thinking as a whole, and the spaces that are between the thoughts. As time moves by, breath-by-breath, you will see the changes as they unfold.

At this point, it might be very sensitive to check the kind of advice you give yourself as you watch the thoughts unfold. It should just be scaffolding. It can just be compared to turning the sound of a TV off, so that you can be watching a match, and you are not being bothered in the unending stream of commentary, and interpretation, and opinion that always characterize the televised sports events.

## The Benefits from Meditation on Thoughts

The first benefit of mindfulness on thoughts is that we will be able to learn about ourselves. There are certain strands of thoughts that just pass through, while other intrigue us, or they just arose our emotions, and so we end up dwelling on them. As we continue to study these thoughts, we will be able to learn about ourselves - our fascinations, fears, desires, attachments, values, habits and others.

We will also be able to discover the subtle thoughts that we usually don't perceive. We will also see how these thoughts feed into our major train of thought, with the unconscious impulses, decision-making, motivations, and a number of other processes. Therefore, we will become more conscious of the other elements that tend to contribute to the whole process of thinking.

Meditation on thoughts will also make us learn about the functioning of the mind in its natural state, when it creates certain thoughts without the conceptual overlays, disruption, and conscious interference. This state of affairs is referred by the Buddhists as the ordinary mind or the natural mind. And, despite the fact that it might appear as ordinary, it is believed to be one of the traits of enlightenment that we have. As we impersonally survey the thought-process, we will get an opportunity to fully disengage from it, and experience consciousness itself.

Some of the guidelines and concepts mentioned here can be used even when we are not performing a formal sitting meditation. It is obviously possible to be aware of our thoughts as we are going through our day-to-day activities that include having conversations, driving, housework, and others more.

We should never try to bring an end to the thought process. This is because it is a natural function of the mind that happens in a continual manner. Should we "try" to squelch our thoughts -before they arrive, or maybe after they have arrived – the 'try" will also be another form of thought, one which will create turbulence and tension as well as a distraction from the meditation itself. We will be able to allow the bodily sensations, feelings, and thoughts to arise, and everything can be easily used as part of our meditation.

Meditation on thought allows us to be aware of the phenomena as opposed to just our thoughts. The phenomena may include the following:

The external sounds – Both the meditation bell and the sound of the cricket will be incorporated into the process of mindfulness meditation, especially as well attain a state in which the terms "internal" and "external" lose their meaning. We will discover that even when a particular even naturally occur, our experience of the event is entirely within ourselves.

For instance, if we hear the sound of a ringing telephone, we look at it, in the same manner, we would look at thought; after all, we are not experiencing an external sound, or the nerve impulses moving to the brain, or the sound wave striking our eardrums, but just an impression in the mind, which might become apparent at the end of the process or even coincide with it.

In most instances, the phenomenon will accompany the thoughts. As the thoughts arise, we will be able to observe the corresponding changes in our muscles, energy, emotions and in the chemistry of our bodies, such as adrenaline releases.

We can be aware of the thoughts by the instant they arrive. If we become aware from the start, we will be able to watch the progression in which a given thought, and the corresponding psychological events, would mechanically proceed into an affiliation with a desire and ultimately into a physical and a stimulus action.

This process also makes it easy for the thoughts to remain in their pre-reflective states. This is basically the state where a thought exists just as an independent entity. Reflection is the procedure where we would control, react, judge, associate, interpret, or identify as we embark on the process of pursuing our thoughts towards a given resolution. Here is where words such as losing ourselves, or thinking about our thinking come up. Prereflection allows us to stay in the moment of clear observation, and we will add absolutely nothing since the thought is already complete on its own.

It would only be our further conceptualizing about the thought that will make it appear inadequate, and it is the same conceptualizing that will be limiting and limited. A perfect example of reflective thought is a sound or a bird, should we hear a chirp outside. Later on, we will release the thought. But if we reflect, we might speculate on the kind of bird, or even wonder if our bird feeder is really full, or even feel annoyed at the supposed distraction that come later on. In our day-to-day life, reflection is an important mode for certain purposes, such as analytical problem solving, but in this kind of meditation, it is just a departure from our main aim.

We shall also observe the impersonal nature of our thoughts. In a single sense, these are just our own thoughts, and so we take full responsibility for them - as a result of the beliefs, mental habits, and prior thoughts, which we have accepted in, as well as the contents of our respective archetypal fields. However, for the sole purpose of exploration, we can still be able to choose an impersonal viewpoint.

First of all, it would be important to note that the thoughts, on their own, are just autonomous objects present in the mental world. Secondly, the thought process is an automatic mechanical operation that obeys the procedures and the dynamics that can't be controlled by the conscious will. From this kind of perspective, we will make the thoughts "think themselves" as opposed to trying ourselves to the thoughts as "my personal thoughts". When meditating, we can pose this important question – "Who is thinking?" The more we learn about the impersonal nature of thoughts; we will become free of them in a number of ways.

Here is just some of them;

We will realize that there is no need of carrying out an action that they would spur. A thought concerning food, for instance, is merely an impersonal thought, implying that it is not something that we are obliged to act out on. We also realize that we don't have to respond in an emotional way to them thought about a controversial topics an impersonal thought, and it is not connected to any particular type of emotional reaction.

We, therefore, realize that we don't have to define ourselves based on the kind of thoughts that we think. A temporary selfish thought, for instance, doesn't mean that we have to adopt the self-image that we are naturally selfish people.

As we continue to study our thoughts, we will realize that some of these thoughts might contradict our self-image (as a shy person, an aggressive person, or a nice person); therefore we must either enlarge the concept of who we are or repress the contradictory thoughts that we have. In the end, the contradictions will compel us to give up the concept of self-concept; and we will instead observe patterns of behavior, and we will find a transcendental self at the end, such as the soul. What this reveals to us is that we are independent to explore our inherent spiritual identity beyond the thought flow, which keep on changing, as opposed to just identifying with any of those thoughts.

We will accept the thought with an attitude that is neutral. All we are doing is just to observe the thoughts, and not to judge them, identifying with them, or even reacting to them. We are also not trying to attach to the thoughts, trying to censor or control them, associate or interpret them.

Should those thoughts of interpretation, association, attachment, control, reaction, and judgment do arise, they are just more thoughts that we will impartially accept as just part of our meditation. Remember that accepting them does not mean that we like them; it just means accepting the reality of it.

When it comes to meditation, we come up with a choiceless awareness, which recognizes, in an objective way, that each thought has equal unimportance or importance. It does not really matter whether a given thought is related to certain objects, or some of the latest experiences. We are only able to perceive our thoughts simply and candidly if we have this kind of neutrality. In the meditation of thoughts, this acceptance is what is known as spaciousness; where we allow space around each thought that we have.

We will be able to observe the thoughts as they progress. It is the nature of thoughts to lead from one to the other. In most cases, the sequence will proceed in this given manner;

We first identify the topic of the thought. We will embark on a memory search to ascertain if we either like or dislike the topic. Based on the liking or disliking, we will then experience what is referred to as aversion, which is a great urge to avoid something.

We shall have obtained a will, or an intention to act upon the aversion or desire

We will then plot a way of securing the objects of desire. Note that the plotting will occur in our intuition, analytical function, or in our habits.

We will then make a physical action to execute this particular plan. Remember that this particular sequence can take place on a mindless unconscious level. For example, we can scratch a particular itch without realizing that we are doing that. Each time we become much aware of the progression as it occurs, we will disengage ourselves from the automatic activity; the step in which to break the progression is always at the main point of intention, where we can intervene and opt to or not act.

We can also override the habitual response so that we can redirect the will toward the goal that we have picked. In the course of meditation, what we generally do is to observe, without having to alter this action's change. But due to the fact that we are not reacting, our mental habits shall not be reinforced as strongly, therefore, we will be at ease to change those habits to the ones that are more productive, and even break from the automatic habit mode status to start enjoying an alertness style, an intuition-based thinking, which is responsible to the dynamics and the needs of the current moment.

The empty state that is between the thoughts will be visible. Many do not realize that thoughts are individual events in the mind, resembling the separate clouds that are floating by in the sky. There is a brief moment that exists between the end of one thought and the beginning of another. This moment can just be perceived when we attune to the cadence of our thoughts –their departure, lingering and departure. Each time we detect that open space between the thoughts, we will be able to enter it and maintain it by being calm attentive to it. In this situation, the mind will be in its natural state of real consciousness.

It is possible to make the thoughts go away without clinging to them. This is the main difference that exists between actively thinking and thoughts. When we have thoughts, they will originate, and linger for some moment, before they pass by. However, we can define thinking as the main process of grabbing a thought and building into it with the following actions – interpretation, association, control, identification, reaction, and judgment. In the process of meditation, we will just observe a thought disappear, in a simple and delicate manner, or just let them be. We will stop fighting the unwanted thoughts, as well as ourselves, since we are aware that the thought will eventually, if we just leave them alone. This sequence is viewed by some group of mediators in several types of analogy. Here are some of them:

The thoughts are seen as logs that are moving down the stream, personally going by, with no absolute connection to each other or no mediator. The only permanence that is present here is the stream itself, and it is very analogous to the consciousness field were the thoughts tend to play themselves out.

The thoughts are then seen as the only frames of movie film, when placed in comparison to the traditional illusion of continuous action.

We are able to view the process by which the thoughts leave a trace of themselves in the various archetypal sectors that we have. Each time we think a given thought, a component of its substance will remain in the archetype field that we are busy pondering.

We can also be much aware of the kind of energy that remains with that particular thought, for instance, the thought could be charged with the emotional energy of love. It is important to note that our karma involves thought patterns as such, and they have been created by our recurring fascinations and desires; a given thought might just appear since we have just encountered as like or a dislike, or another reaction to a previous thought of that nature.

That previous personal reaction would leave an energetic charge, which will make the related thoughts to appear; therefore, there is no point in trying to hold back any thought topic. This is due to the fact that it is the expression of the previously created karma. In the meditative process of the detached observation, we will notice thoughts without any personal reaction; therefore we will not come up with any additional charged thoughts. In addition to that, we will also allow the previous charges to dissipate such that we get freedom from the habitual patterns of thought.

Of course, we will still create other habits since one of the main functions of the mind is to create habits, but we might just realize that any new habits will be less ingrained since our new approach to situations is more creative, spontaneous, sensitively responsive to that kind of circumstance as opposed to being automatic in its reliance upon the habits that are already in existence.

## Conclusion

I am extremely excited to pass this information along to you, and I am so happy that you now have read and can hopefully implement these strategies going forward.

I hope this book was able to help you understand the complexities of human self-compassion and how to develop and use it for the improvement of your life.

The next step is to get started using this information and to hopefully live a confident, optimistic, and self-compassionate life!

Please don't be someone who just reads this information and doesn't apply it, the strategies in this book will only benefit you if you use them!

If you know of anyone else that could benefit from the information presented here please inform them of this book.

Thank you and good luck!

www.ingramcontent.com/pod-product-compliance
Lightning Source LLC
Chambersburg PA
CBHW072005070526
44583CB00015B/1340